Ethan V. Munson   Charles Nicholas
Derick Wood (Eds.)

Principles of Digital Document Processing

4th International Workshop, PODDP'98
Saint Malo, France, March 29-30, 1998
Proceedings

Springer

Series Editors

Gerhard Goos, Karlsruhe University, Germany
Juris Hartmanis, Cornell University, NY, USA
Jan van Leeuwen, Utrecht University, The Netherlands

Volume Editors

Ethan V. Munson
University of Wisconsin-Milwaukee
Department of Electrical Engineering and Computer Science
Milwaukee, WI 53211, USA
E-mail: munson@cs.uwm.edu

Charles Nicholas
University of Maryland, Baltimore County
Department of Computer Science and Electrical Engineering
1000 Hilltop Circle, Baltimore, MD 21250, USA
E-mail: nicholas@cs.umbc.edu

Derick Wood
Hong Kong University of Science and Technology
Department of Computer Science
Clear Water Bay, Kowloon, Hong Kong SAR
E-mail: dwood@cs.ust.hk

Cataloging-in-Publication data applied for

Die Deutsche Bibliothek - CIP-Einheitsaufnahme

Principles of digital document processing : 4th international
workshop ; proceedings / PODDP '98, Saint Malo, France, March
29 - 30, 1998. Ethan V. Munson ... (ed.). - Berlin ; Heidelberg ; New
York ; Barcelona ; Budapest ; Hong Kong ; London ; Milan ; Paris ;
Singapore ; Tokyo : Springer, 1998
  (Lecture notes in computer science ; Vol. 1481)
  ISBN 3-540-65086-5

CR Subject Classification (1991): I.7, H.5, I.3.7, I.4, H.2.8

ISSN 0302-9743
ISBN 3-540-65086-5 Springer-Verlag Berlin Heidelberg New York

© Springer-Verlag Berlin Heidelberg 1998
Printed in Germany

Typesetting: Camera-ready by author
SPIN 10638766   06/3142 – 5 4 3 2 1 0   Printed on acid-free paper

QA 66 S LEC/1481

Lecture Notes in Computer Science 1481
Edited by G. Goos, J. Hartmanis and J. van Leeuwen

Springer

Berlin
Heidelberg
New York
Barcelona
Budapest
Hong Kong
London
Milan
Paris
Singapore
Tokyo

Preface

The Fourth International Workshop on Principles of Digital Document Processing took place in Saint Malo, France on March 29 and 30, 1998. PODDP'98 was the fourth in a series of international workshops that provide forums to discuss the modeling of document processing systems using theories and techniques from, for example, computer science, mathematics, and psychology. PODDP'98 took place in conjunction with EP'98 at the Palais des Congrès in Saint Malo.

The charter of PODDP is deliberately ambitious and its scope broad. Indeed, we have added the adjective "Digital" to the series title to reflect the workshop's emphasis on multimedia documents. The current state of digital document systems can be characterized as a plethora of tools without a clear articulation of unifying principles and underlying concepts. The practical and commercial impact of these tools — editors and formatters for many media (text, graphics, video, audio, animation), composition systems, digital libraries, the World Wide Web, word processing systems, structured editors, document management systems — is too pervasive and obvious to require further elaboration and emphasis.

With the rapid development in hardware technology (processors, memory, and high bandwidth networks), however, the notion of a document and of document processing itself is undergoing a profound change. The growing use of multimedia has expanded our notions about content, scale, and dynamicity of documents. To address these changes, we hope to bring to bear theories and techniques developed by researchers in other areas of science, mathematics, engineering and the humanities (such as databases, formal specification languages and methodologies, optimization, workflow analysis, and user interface design).

The PODDP workshops are intended to promote a happy marriage between documents and document processing, and theories and techniques. PODDP provides an ideal opportunity for discussion and information exchange between researchers who are grappling with problems in *any* area of document processing.

We invited researchers to submit papers with a good balance between theory and practice in document processing. Papers that addressed both on a somewhat equal basis were preferred. Each paper was subjected to rigorous peer review.

Finally, we hope that the work presented in this volume will stimulate other researchers to join us in investigating the principles of digital document processing. To support the dissemination of this research, plans are being made for the next workshop in this series, PODDP 2000, to be held in conjunction with DDEP 2000, the Eighth International Conference on Digital Documents and Electronic Publishing.

July 1998

Ethan V. Munson
Charles Nicholas
Derick Wood

Organization

Steering Committee

Derick Wood (Hong Kong University of Science & Technology), Chair
Anne Brueggemann-Klein (Technische Universität München, Germany)
Richard Furuta (Texas A&M University, USA)
Ethan V. Munson (University of Wisconsin-Milwaukee, USA)
Makoto Murata (Fuji Xerox Informations Co. Ltd., Japan)
Charles Nicholas (University of Maryland, Baltimore County, USA)

Program Committee

Charles Nicholas (University of Maryland, Baltimore County, USA), Co-Chair
Derick Wood (Hong Kong University of Science & Technology), Co-Chair
Howard Blair (Syracuse University, USA)
Heather Brown (University of Kent-Canterbury, UK)
Anne Brueggemann-Klein (Technische Universität München, Germany)
Norbert Fuhr (Universität Dortmund, Germany)
Richard Furuta (Texas A&M University, USA)
Heikki Mannila (University of Helsinki, Finland)
Ethan V. Munson (University of Wisconsin-Milwaukee, USA)
Makoto Murata (Fuji Xerox Information Systems, Japan)
Cecile Roisin (INRIA Rhône-Alpes, France)

Table of Contents

Context and Caterpillars and Structured Documents*

Anne Brüggemann-Klein[1], Stefan Hermann[1], and Derick Wood[2]

[1] Institut für Informatik, Technische Universität München, Arcisstr. 21, 80290
München, Germany.
E-mail: {brueggem, hermann}@informatik.tu-muenchen.de.
WWW: http://www11.informatik.tu-muenchen.de.
[2] Department of Computer Science, Hong Kong University of Science & Technology,
Clear Water Bay, Kowloon, Hong Kong.
E-mail: dwood@cs.ust.hk.
WWW: http://www.cs.ust.hk/~dwood.

Abstract. We present a novel, yet simple, technique for the specification
of context in structured documents that we call caterpillar expressions.
Although we are applying this technique in the specification of context-
dependent style sheets for HTML, XML, and SGML documents, it is
clear that it can be used in other environments such as query specification
for structured documents and for computer program transformations.
In addition, we present a number of theoretical results that allow us to
compare the expressive power of caterpillar expressions to that of tree
automata.

1 Introduction

Context-dependent processing and specification are not new topics; they surface
in almost all computing activities. What is somewhat surprising is that the issue
of context as a topic in its own right does not appear to have been studied. In
the DESIGNER project, that we have been working on over a number of years,
we were faced with the problem of the specification of context-dependent style
rules. At first, we expected to use the traditional approach from the compiler
and programming-languages community; namely, attribution [2, 12, 21]. In addition, we also expected to be able to use and modify previous approaches to style
specification such as suggested by the DSSSL document [3] and Lie's work [14,
15] for SGML [10] and XML [8] style specification. Alternatively, we considered
Munson's approach in the Proteus system [19] and Murata's more general approach [20] which uses a tree-automata-based approach. Murata's approach is the
closest technique to ours, although more traditional and quite different. But, we
were faced with an additional constraint that changed our thinking. We wanted

---

* The work of the three authors was supported partially by a joint DAAD-HK grant.
In addition, the work of the third author was supported under a grant from the
Research Grants Council of Hong Kong.

to provide a system for graphics designers to use to specify style rules and style sheets [5]. The point here is that they would be primarily computer naive. They would almost certainly find the manipulation of attributes difficult. Therefore, we decided to separate, somewhat, the specification of context from the issue of style specification. One observation about this separation is in order: we need only provide a mechanism that tests whether a specific context of a given part of a document is present or not. Based on this observation, the style rules may now incorporate conditional statements or expressions to express context-dependent choices. Thus, we can isolate context determination from style rule syntax to a large extent. The preliminary work on DESIGNER did just that [4, 7]. We have also investigated style-sheet specification for tables [23] and investigated some basic decidability questions for style sheets [6].

The contextual technique we introduce is also applicable to the compilation of computer programs, but is of less interest there as compiler designers and writers do not allow users to modify a compiler according to new context dependencies. We might use these techniques when developing code optimizers or other program transformation tools since, with both examples, there may be a number of individuals collaborating on the development [18].

Once we have isolated the specification of contexts from the more general specification of style sheets, we are able to provide naive users with better support for this aspect of style specification. Indeed, it also frees us to consider different techniques (different from attribution, for example) for context specification. Since regular expressions are understood by many people who are not programmers *per se,* and they are the simplest specification technique, we decided to use them for context specification. Mendelzon's research [9, 16] has shown, with his graph-theoretic query language G++ for databases, that this approach is not only powerful but also it can be visualized well [9]. (In Mendelzon's project, users provide restrictions of a graph-theoretic view of a database by graph-theoretic means. This visual process provides, essentially, a subgraph as the query.) Similar approaches have been used by Lauer *et al.* [13] to specify paths and processes for concurrent systems.

We make the well-accepted assumption that a set of similar documents are modeled by syntax trees or abstract syntax trees of a given grammar (an SGML DTD, an XML DTD or HTML) that generates the set of all such documents.

2   Caterpillars and Context

It is natural to write of a context c of a node u; for example, if u is a paragraph, we may wish to determine whether u is the first paragraph of a chapter or of a section. In this setting, the property "is the first paragraph of a chapter or of a section" is the context. We choose to invert this intuitive notion by identifying all first paragraphs in chapters and sections of a document as the context "first paragraph." Thus, for a specific abstract syntax tree, the set of first-paragraph-in-a-chapter-or-in-a-section nodes are the context "first paragraph." In other words, for a given tree T, each set S of nodes of T may be a context in the sense that the nodes in S are all the nodes in T that, intuitively, have a specific context.

Since a real caterpillar crawls around a tree, we define a **contextual caterpillar** as a sequence of atomic movements and atomic tests. A caterpillar can move from the current node to its parent, to its left sibling, to its right sibling, to its first child, or to its last child. To prevent a caterpillar from dropping off a tree it is allowed to test whether it is at a leaf (external node), at the root, at the first sibling, or at the last sibling. Note that these navigational and testing operations define an ADT for trees; however, caterpillars are more than an ADT as they capture a specific sequence of ADT operations.

For example, given the partial document tree in Fig. 1, a first-paragraph-in-chapter caterpillar is:

$$p, \mathtt{isfirst}, \mathtt{up}, \mathtt{up}, \mathtt{up}, \mathtt{ch},$$

where a node label is an implicit test on the current node, and a first-paragraph-in-section caterpillar is:

$$p, \mathtt{isfirst}, \mathtt{up}, \mathtt{up}, \mathtt{up}, \mathtt{up}, \mathtt{sect}.$$

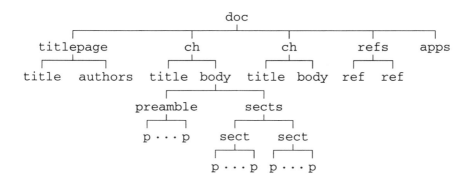

Fig. 1. An example document tree.

Similarly, a last-section caterpillar is:

$$\mathtt{sect}, \mathtt{islast}.$$

In each of these examples, if we place the caterpillar at any node in a given tree, it crawls and evaluates until it has executed the sequence successfully, it cannot carry out the next move, or it has obtained a false evaluation of a test. Clearly, this notion of a caterpillar's evaluation leads to a set of nodes in a tree that are the context of the caterpillar.

In general, we want to be able to specify contexts for all trees of a given grammar or SGML DTD and we may not be able to do so with a single caterpillar. For example, consider document trees in which emphasized text can be nested (as it can be in LaTeX); see Fig. 2. Typically, we emphasize text in a

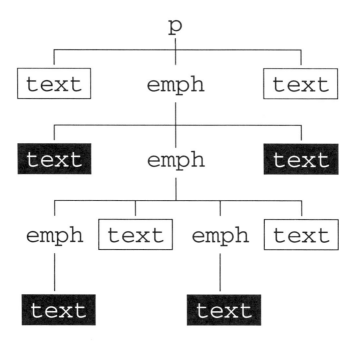

Fig. 2. A document tree with nested emphasized text.

roman environment by setting it in italic whereas we emphasize text in an italic environment by setting it in roman. Thus, we need to determine the parity of the nesting to be able to specify the appropriate typeface.

The caterpillar

$$\text{text}, \text{up}, \text{p}$$

and the caterpillar

$$\text{text}, \text{up}, \text{emph}, \text{up}, \text{emph}, \text{up}, \text{p}$$

specify contexts with even parity whereas the caterpillars:

$$\text{text}, \text{up}, \text{emph}, \text{up}, \text{p}$$

and

$$\mathtt{text, up, emph, up, emph, up, emph, up, p}$$

specify odd-parity contexts in the tree of Fig. 2.

We need, however, to specify caterpillars of any length as the depth of emphasis nesting is not bounded, even though it is finite. The solution is simple, yet powerful.

Rather than allowing only a finite number of caterpillars for each context, we allow infinite sets of caterpillars. Since we can consider a caterpillar to be a string over the set of tests and nonterminals (or elements) of the grammars, a set of caterpillars is a language in the usual language-theoretic sense.

We use regular expressions, called **caterpillar expressions,** to specify such languages, called **caterpillar languages,** and we use finite-state machines to model their execution. For example, we specify all even-parity-emphasis contexts for trees of the form given in Fig. 2 by the following caterpillar expression:

$$\mathtt{text} \cdot [\mathtt{up} \cdot \mathtt{emph} \cdot \mathtt{up} \cdot \mathtt{emph}]^* \cdot \mathtt{up} \cdot \mathtt{p}$$

and the odd-parity-emphasis contexts as follows:

$$\mathtt{text} \cdot \mathtt{up} \cdot \mathtt{emph} \cdot [\mathtt{up} \cdot \mathtt{emph} \cdot \mathtt{up} \cdot \mathtt{emph}]^* \cdot \mathtt{up} \cdot \mathtt{p}.$$

Our method of specifying contexts singles out those nodes in the trees of a grammar for which the execution of one of the caterpillars in the given caterpillar language evaluates to true when started on these nodes. One immediate implication of this model is that we must separately specify even-parity contexts and even-parity contexts since we need to specify different actions in each case.

3   Caterpillar Expressions and Tree Automata

We provide the formal definition of caterpillars and caterpillar languages, and demonstrate how we can model their execution with tree automata. Merk [17] has investigated some of the basic properties of caterpillar expressions.

Document trees (or abstract syntax trees) have node labels from an alphabet Σ. Since we view SGML (and grammatical) documents as trees, element names (or nonterminals) are the node labels. The content of a document is represented as an external node or leaf of such a tree whose label is also in Σ. Each SGML DTD (or document grammar) defines a set of trees $\mathcal{T}$. Not every set of trees we are discussing needs to be defined by an SGML DTD though. Given a set $\mathcal{T}$, a context $\mathcal{C}$ for $\mathcal{T}$ maps any tree T in $\mathcal{T}$ to a subset $\mathcal{C}(T)$ of $nodes(T)$. Hence, we say that a node v of T is in the context $\mathcal{C}$ or belongs to $\mathcal{C}$ if and only if $v \in \mathcal{C}(T)$. In other words, $\mathcal{C}(T)$ denotes the nodes of T that are in context $\mathcal{C}$.

Let Δ denote the alphabet of moves and tests; that is,

$$\Delta = \{\mathtt{up}, \mathtt{left}, \mathtt{right}, \mathtt{first}, \mathtt{last}, \mathtt{isfirst}, \mathtt{islast}, \mathtt{isleaf}, \mathtt{isroot}\}.$$

A string x over $\Sigma \cup \Delta$ is a caterpillar and it denotes a context c_x for the set of Σ-labeled trees as follows. For any tree T and any node v of T:

- if $x = \lambda$, then v belongs to c_λ.
- if $x = aw$, where $a \in \Sigma \cup \Delta$ and $w \in (\Sigma \cup \Delta)^*$, v belongs to c_{aw} if and only if one of the following conditions holds:
  1. a is in Σ, v has label a and v belongs to c_w.
  2. $a = \texttt{up}$, v has a parent $u \in T$ and u belongs to c_w.
  3. $a = \texttt{left}$, v has a direct left sibling $u \in T$ and u belongs to c_w.
  4. $a = \texttt{right}$, v has a direct right sibling $u \in T$ and u belongs to c_w.
  5. $a = \texttt{first}$, v has children in T and v's leftmost child is u and u belongs to c_w.
  6. $a = \texttt{last}$, v has children in T and v's rightmost child is u and u belongs to c_w.
  7. $a = \texttt{isfirst}$, v is the leftmost node among its siblings in T and v belongs to c_w.
  8. $a = \texttt{islast}$, v is the rightmost node among its siblings in T and v belongs to c_w.
  9. $a = \texttt{isleaf}$, v is an external node in T and v belongs to c_w.
  10. $a = \texttt{isroot}$, v is the root node of T and v belongs to c_w.

Note that this formal definition of the meaning of a caterpillar corresponds to the informal notion we used in the previous section.

A language L over the alphabet $\Sigma \cup \Delta$ also denotes a context, namely

$$c_L = \bigcup_{x \in L} c_x.$$

Hence, a node v of a tree T is in the context c_L of language L if, starting from v, it is possible to perform at least one sequence $x \in L$ of moves and tests in T.

We call $\Sigma \cup \Delta$ the caterpillar alphabet of Σ. A language, regular expression or finite-state machine over a caterpillar alphabet is called a caterpillar language, a caterpillar expression, or a caterpillar machine, respectively. We now restrict our attention to **regular caterpillar languages** (languages defined by caterpillar expressions) and to **regular caterpillar contexts** (contexts defined by regular caterpillar languages). We can define how caterpillar machines operate on trees basing the definition on sequences of configurations in the standard manner. A configuration in this case consists of a node of a tree (the current node), a state of the machine (the current state), and a string x over the caterpillar alphabet (the remaining input string).

Theorem 1. *Given a tree T with m nodes and a caterpillar machine M with n transitions, we can compute the set of nodes in T that are in the context $c_{L(M)}$ in time $O(m \cdot n)$.*

We can define tree automata using the approach of Thatcher [22]. The key point about his approach is that the node labels are not ranked, any node label may label any node in a tree independently of the number of children that node has. We omit the formal definition of tree automata here since it is well documented in the literature and the definition is technically laborious even though the concept is simple.

We use a variant of tree automata called **endmarked tree automata** which are tree automata with two designated labels $\top$ and $\bot$ that are used as endmarkers for the trees it processes.

A tree T with endmarkers has labels from an alphabet Σ that contains the endmarkers $\top$ and $\bot$; furthermore, T must be labeled in such a way that:

1. The root of T is labeled $\top$.
2. Each external node is labeled $\bot$.
3. The root is has only one child.
4. External nodes have no siblings.
5. All other nodes in T are labeled with symbols from $\Sigma - \{\top, \bot\}$.

Tree automata come in two flavors: bottom-up tree automata and top-down tree automata. In addition, they can be deterministic or nondeterministic. The following results are well known.

Proposition 1. *For every tree language L, L is accepted by a nondeterministic bottom-up tree automaton if and only if it is accepted by a nondeterministic top-down tree automaton.*

Proposition 2. *For every tree language L, L is accepted by a nondeterministic bottom-up tree automaton if and only if it is accepted by a deterministic bottom-up tree automaton.*

This result does not hold for top-down tree automata.

To explore the relationship between regular caterpillar languages and tree automata we introduce the notion of **caterpillar tree-regular languages.** A language L of trees is a caterpillar tree-regular language if there is a regular caterpillar context c such that T is in L if and only if the root of T is in the context c. We state the following new results without proof:

Theorem 2. *For each extended context-free grammar, the set of its syntax trees is a caterpillar tree-regular language.*

Theorem 3. *Each finite tree language is caterpillar tree regular.*

Theorem 4. *There are (finite) caterpillar tree-regular languages that cannot be accepted by any deterministic top-down tree automaton.*

Theorem 5. *A finite union of caterpillar tree-regular languages is also a caterpillar tree-regular language.*

Given a string language L, it denotes a tree language $RF(L)$, the **root-to-frontier language of L,** as follows: A tree T is in $RF(L)$ if and only if the labels of each root-to-frontier path in T form a string in L.

Theorem 6. *If L is a regular string language, then its root-to-frontier tree language $RF(L)$ is a caterpillar tree-regular language.*

We now state, again without proofs, the results that demonstrate that caterpillar tree languages are deterministic bottom-up tree-automaton languages. We prove this result indirectly using two-way nondeterministic tree automata. In such automata, the computation starts at the frontier of a tree and terminates at the root as with bottom-up tree automata, but in addition it also allows the computation to locally move up or down the tree. The similarity to two-way finite-state machines should be clear.

Theorem 7. *Each caterpillar tree-regular language is accepted by a two-way nondeterministic automaton.*

Finally, we can emulate two-way tree automata with bottom-up tree automata to give the last result.

Theorem 8. *Each caterpillar tree-regular language is accepted by a deterministic bottom-up tree automaton.*

4   Closing Remarks

We can reprove two of Kilpeläinen's results [11] about tree inclusion problems using the notion of caterpillar context. The proofs are simpler and more uniform than Kilpeläinen's original proofs.

Lastly, a number of readers of the first draft of this paper mentioned the similarity to the programming language developed in the Logo Group of the MIT Artificial Intelligence Laboratory [1]. It was designed to explore mathematics by students who ranged in age from preschool to postdoctoral. One of the cute aspects of the language is the use of turtle geometry to investigate geometrical notions. It was called turtle geometry because a user manipulated a "turtle" (a representation of the cursor's current position) with a simple command-based language. Children, and even adults, were able to draw complex figures very quickly using the turtle as metaphor and guide. We hope that our use of caterpillars will garner a similar response from graphics designers.

References

1. H. Abelson and A.A. diSessa. *Turtle Geometry: The Computer as Medium for Exploring Mathematics.* MIT Press, Cambridge, MA, 1980.
2. H. Alblas and B. Melichar. *Attribute Grammars, Applications and Systems.* Springer-Verlag, Heidelberg, 1991. LNCS 545.
3. J. Bosak. Web page on DSSSL online. http://sunsite.unc.edu/pub/sun-info/standards/dsssl/dssslo/do960816.htm, 1997.
4. A. Brüggemann-Klein. Formal models in document processing. Habilitationsschrift. Faculty of Mathematics at the University of Freiburg, 1993.
5. A. Brüggemann-Klein and S. Hermann. Design by Example: A user-centered approach to the specification of document layout. In F. Rowland and J. Meadows, editors, *Electronic Publishing '97: New Models and Opportunities. Proceedings of an ICCC/IFIP Conference held at the University of Kent at Canterbury, England, 14-16 April 1997*, pages 223–236. ICCC Press, 1997. URL: http://www11.informatik.tu-muenchen.de/proj/designer/canterbury.ps.

6. A. Brüggemann-Klein and T. Schroff. Grammar-compatible stylesheets. In C. Nicholas and D. Wood, editors, *Proceedings of the Third International Workshop on Principles of Document Processing (PODP 96)*, pages 51–58, Heidelberg, 1996. Springer-Verlag. Lecture Notes of Computer Science 1293.

7. A. Brüggemann-Klein and D. Wood. Electronic style sheets. Interner Bericht 45, Institut für Informatik, Universität Freiburg, January 1992.

8. D. Connolly. W3C web page on XML. http://www.w3.org/XML/, 1997.

9. M. P. Consens, F. C. Eigler, M. Z. Hasan, A. O. Mendelzon, E. G. Naik, A. G. Ryman, and D. Vista. Architecture and application of the Hy+ visualization system. *IBM Systems Journal*, 33(3):458–476, 1994.

10. ISO 8879: Information processing—Text and office systems—Standard Generalized Markup Language (SGML), October 1986. International Organization for Standardization.

11. P. Kilpeläinen and H. Mannila. Grammatical tree matching. Report C-1991-61, Department of Computer Science, University of Helsinki, Finland, 1991.

12. D. E. Knuth. Semantics of context-free languages. *Mathematical Systems Theory*, 2(2):127–145, 1968.

13. P. E. Lauer, P. R. Torrigiani, and M. W. Shields. COSY: A system specification language based on paths and processes. *Acta Informatica*, 12:109–158, 1979.

14. H. Lie. W3C web page on Cascading Style Sheets. http://www.w3.org/Style/css/, 1997.

15. H. Lie and B. Bos. *Cascading Style Sheets: Designing for the Web*. Addison-Wesley Publishing Company, Reading, MA, 1998.

16. A. O. Mendelzon and P. T. Wood. Finding regular simple paths in graph databases. *SIAM Journal of Computing*, 24(6), December 1995.

17. M. Merk. Spezifikation von Mustern als Kontexte. Master's thesis, Institut für Informatik, Universität Freiburg, 1994.

18. John David Morgenthaler. *Static Analysis for a Software Transformation Tool*. PhD thesis, University of California, San Diego, Department of Computer Science and Engineering, 1997. Also available as Technical Report CS97-552 and from URL: http://www-cse.ucsd.edu/users/jdm/Papers/Dissertation.html.

19. E. V. Munson. *Proteus: An Adaptable Presentation System for a Software Development and Multimedia Document Environment*. PhD thesis, Computer Science Division, University of California, Berkeley, 1994.

20. M. Murata. Transformation of documents and schemas by patterns and contextual conditions. In C. Nicholas and D. Wood, editors, *Proceedings of the Third International Workshop on Principles of Document Processing (PODP 96)*, pages 153–169, Heidelberg, 1997. Springer-Verlag. Lecture Notes in Computer Science 1293.

21. W. Schreiber. *Generierung von Dokumentverarbeitungssystemen aus formalen Spezifikationen von Dokumentarchitekturen*. PhD thesis, Institut für Informatik, Technische Universität München, 1996.

22. J.W. Thatcher. Characterizing derivation trees of context-free grammars through a generalization of finite automata theory. *Journal of Computer and System Sciences*, 1:317–322, 1967.

23. X. Wang and D. Wood. Xtable—A tabular editor and formatter. In A. Brown, A. Brüggemann-Klein, and A. Feng, editors, *EP96, Proceedings of the Sixth International Conference on Electronic Publishing, Document Manipulation and Typography*, pages 167–180, 1996. Special Issue, Electronic Publishing—Origination, Dissemination and Design 8(2 and 3).

A Conceptual Model for Tables*

Xinxin Wang[1] and Derick Wood[2]

[1] AT&T Labs, 200 Laurel Avenue, Middletown, NJ 07748, USA.
`xinxin@puma.att.com`.
[2] Department of Computer Science, Hong Kong University of Science & Technology,
Clear Water Bay, Kowloon, Hong Kong.
`dwood@cs.ust.hk`.
WWW: `http://www.cs.ust.hk/~dwood`.

Abstract. We describe a new, simple conceptual model for tables. The conceptual model treats a table as a map that has a domain which is a product of categories or index sets and a codomain which is a set of entry values. We demonstrate how we can use the model to specify the semantics of some tabular editing operations.

1 Introduction

Tables have been and are primarily a presentational technique, but with the surge of use of the Internet and computers, we expect that tables will be used even more. Moreover, they will be used in new ways. For example, tables are already being produced that are much too large to be displayed on a single page or in a single window. In this scenario, we need to have a sound conceptual model of tables to provide a foundation for the design of tabular browsers, the production of tabular views, and the design of tabular query systems.

The ideas we discuss are presented in a more rudimentary form in Wang's thesis [21] and in even more rudimentary form in an early paper by Wang and Wood [22]. Vanoirbeek [19, 20] appears to have been the first researcher to identify the multidimensional nature of tables and the hierarchical structure of rubrics, which we call categories or index sets depending on the context. Tables present a challenging problem for structured-document modelers as they do not fit comfortably in a hierarchical model as Furuta [10] observed in his thesis. Models that are more presentation oriented have been discussed by others [2, 3, 5, 7, 16, 17, 15] as well by the SGML community [12–14]. We could, of course, use a more complex apparatus for modeling tables, such as type theory or algebraic specifications, but our stance and philosophy is to develop small models using simple notions, rather than base models on more complex notions. This approach is similar to the "small languages" approach of Jon Bentley, Brian Kernighan and others [4], and to the "KIS" philosophy of system and program design. Brooks [6] explores what may and will happen when systems are large and are complex.

---

* This work was supported under a grant from the Research Grants Council of Hong Kong.

The **content** of a table is a collection of interrelated items that may be numbers, text, symbols, figures, mathematical equations, or even other tables. There are two kinds of items: the basic data displayed by a table, the **entries,** and the auxiliary data used to locate the entries, the **labels.** For example, Table 1 presents the average marks for the assignments and examinations of a course offered in the three terms of 1991 and 1992. The marks are the entries (for

Table 1. The average marks for 1991–1992.

	Assignments			Examinations		Grade
	Ass1	Ass2	Ass3	Midterm	Final	
1991						
Winter	85	80		60	75	75
Spring	80	65	75	60	70	70
Fall	80	85		55	80	75
1992						
Winter	85	80		70	75	75
Spring	80	80			75	75
Fall	75	70	65	60	80	70

example, 75 and 80) and the strings that denote the years, the terms, and the kinds of marks are the labels (for example, 1991, Winter, and Midterm). We cannot always determine what are labels and what are entries so easily; however, we shall assume we can always do so and that they are disjoint from each other.

A table is divided into four main regions by **stub separation** and **boxhead separation.** The **stub** is the lower left region that contains the row headings, the **boxhead** is the upper right region that contains the column headings, the **stub head** is the upper left region that contains the index sets in the stub, and the **body** is the region to the right of the stub and below the boxhead that contains the entries.

We present a conceptual model for tables that is based on simple mathematical notions. It is presentation independent (it does not depend on any specific display of a table), representation independent (we do not provide any specific representation of the model), and it is system independent (it is isolated from any tabular management system). As an application of the model, we demonstrate how it can be used to specify the semantics of some tabular editing operations. a tabular editor. We consider our tabular model to be a first step in addressing the problem: "What is a table?" It bears a similar relationship to tables that a context-free grammar model has to programming languages—there is much left unsaid. Despite this frugality, the model provides a firm basis for further work.

2 Some Preliminary Remarks

We present a conceptual model for tables that captures the underlying syntactic
relationships of a table. The conceptual model treats a table as a map that has
an unordered Cartesian product of categories or index sets as its domain and
some universe of entries as its codomain. The index sets are restricted partial
orders; indeed, they are trees. The number of index sets determines the dimension of the table and, as with programming language arrays, each entry in a
d-dimensional table is determined by d indices. The method of indexing tables is
what makes tables different from arrays and spreadsheets. We base the tabular
model on a formalism for categories and index sets that is appropriate for tables.
Our position is that the manipulation of categories is the primary aspect of tabular manipulation whether it is for editing, querying, or formatting. In contrast,
index sets for arrays and spreadsheets do not use and do not require such a rich
repertoire of index-set operations.

One way we use a table such as Table 1 is that we have a specific year, term,
and kind of mark in mind and we want to retrieve the corresponding mark. For
example, the mark corresponding to 1992, Spring, Examinations, and Final is
75. We use the labels to index a unique entry. Observe that although the label
Spring occurs twice in the table, we use only one of its appearances; namely, the
one within 1992. There is a hierarchical arrangement of years and terms in this
table; in general, tabular labels are arranged hierarchically. We use dot notation
to indicate the hierarchical dependence by writing 1992·Spring as the stub index
(Dewey decimal classification schemes, email addresses, and C++ structures use
a similar notation). Similarly, Midterm and Final both depend on Examinations,
so we write Examinations·Final as the box-head index. Dependent labels define
indices and sets of indices form **index sets**, which are hierarchical. Table 1 has
six stub indices and six box-head indices, so the table has 36 entries (although
some identical entries are presented only once) and its **size** is, therefore, 36.

Presentationally, a table is two-dimensional; hence, two indices are necessary
and sufficient to determine a unique entry. Conceptually, however, Table 1 may
be viewed as a three-dimensional table since Year and Term may be treated as
separate index sets. (Observe that we cannot break Marks into two or more index
sets.) In this case, we need three indices to determine an entry uniquely just as
we do with a three-dimensional array. Observe that there are two Year, three
Term, and six Marks indices, so the conceptual table still has size $2 \times 3 \times 6 = 36$.
As a reader, we use a Cartesian product (even when we do not think of it this
way) of the three index sets

$$Year = \{1991, 1992\},$$

$$Term = \{Winter, Spring, Fall\},$$

and

$$Marks = \{Assignments \cdot Ass1, Assignments \cdot Ass2, Assignments \cdot Ass3,$$

$$Examinations \cdot Midterm, Examinations \cdot Final, Grade\}$$

to specify the entries. There are six possible products, the one in Table 1 is the product $Year \times Term \times Marks$. The other five different products are $Year \times Marks \times Term$, $Term \times Year \times Marks$, $Term \times Marks \times Year$, $Marks \times Term \times Year$, and $Marks \times Year \times Term$. The different products correspond to the same conceptual table presented in different ways. In addition, for each product of the three indices, we can assign the index sets to the stub and boxhead in four different ways. For example, the partition given in Table 1 is $Year \times Term\| \times Marks$, where we use '$\|$' to specify the partition (this notation is similar to, but different from, the use of parentheses suggested by Darrell Raymond [18]). We could use one of the other three partitions $\|Year \times Term \times Marks$, $Year\| \times Term \times Marks$, or $Year \times Term \times Marks\|$.

An array is a random-access data structure for efficient storage and retrieval. For example, the array $R[0..1, 0..2, 0..3]$ of real numbers is three-dimensional and it has $2 \times 3 \times 4 = 24$ elements whose values are real numbers. The array R can be modeled as a map from a Cartesian product of the three index sets to the reals.

Tables and arrays (and spreadsheets) have, not surprisingly, some similarities: Both can be multidimensional and both are indexed by products of index sets. But at this point the similarities end and we find only differences.

Product order: Each Cartesian product of the index sets of an array determines a different array. For example, for the array R, we have the product order $0..1 \times 0..2 \times 0..3$. If we change the product order to $0..2 \times 0..1 \times 0..3$, say, it is a different array.

For tables, each different product order determines the same table with a different presentation.

Index sets: The ordering of the indices in an index set is total for arrays, but for tables it may be a total order, a partial order, a preorder, or no order at all. In addition, array index sets are not only a total order but also they are a subrange of a total order (usually the set of integers). For example, for the array R, $0..3$ is a subrange of the integers, but the index set $\{Winter, Spring, Fall\}$ is not a subrange of the understood total order $\{Winter, Spring, Summer, Fall\}$. The index set for Marks is a partial order but is not a total order as $Midterm$ has no predefined relationship with assignments $Ass1$, $Ass2$, and $Ass3$.

Use: Arrays are a data structure for the efficient storage and retrieval of similar kinds of values. They provide random access to the stored values. Tables, on the other hand, are a structure for the presentation and effective retrieval of data; presentation is their primary use, whereas presentation is at most a secondary use for arrays.

The manipulation of tables is, therefore, necessarily more complex than is the manipulation of arrays. We want to be able to change the product ordering, the partition of the index sets between the stub and the box head, and the ordering within index sets to achieve the purpose of a specific table—*to communicate information and its relationships.*

3   The Conceptual Model

We use strings and dotted strings to define index sets for tables. We have chosen dotted strings simply because we want to incorporate the categorial labels directly in the dotted strings. We then use unordered Cartesian products of index sets and maps to obtain the tabular model.

Let Σ be an alphabet of symbols and $A \subseteq \Sigma^*$ be a finite set of strings over Σ. Then, a **dotted string** x over A is the **null dotted string** that we denote by Λ, is a string in A, or $x = y \cdot z$, where y is in A and z is a dotted string over A. For example, $Winter \cdot 1994$ is a dotted string over the set $\{1993, 1994, Fall, Winter, Spring\}$. The dotted string Λ satisfies the usual properties of a nullity: $x \cdot \Lambda = \Lambda \cdot x = x$, for all dotted strings x. Indices are dotted strings and index sets are sets of dotted strings that satisfy a simple, yet important, property. Given a dotted string x, a dotted string y is a **dotted prefix** of x if $x = y \cdot z$ for some dotted string z. Clearly, a dotted string is always a dotted prefix of itself and Λ is a dotted prefix of every dotted string.

A set X of dotted strings is **prefix free** if, for each dotted string x in X, there is no dotted string $y \in X$ such that $x \neq y$ and $x = y \cdot z$, for some dotted string z. The crucial point about a prefix-free set X of dotted strings is that it can be represented by a tree in which the root is labeled with Λ, each nonroot node is labeled with a string from A, and each root-to-frontier path spells out an index string in X. (We may alternatively choose to label each edge with a string from A and the conceptual incoming edge of the root with Λ.) We define an **index set** to be a prefix-free dotted-string set.

We are now in a position to define our tabular model. A **table** is defined by three items: A finite collection $\mathcal{I} = \{I_1, \ldots\}$ of index sets, a universe $\mathcal{E}$ of entry values, and a map τ from the unordered Cartesian product of the index sets to the universe of entry values. In other words, we have $\tau : \bigotimes \mathcal{I} \longrightarrow \mathcal{E}$. Thus, we use a tuple $(\mathcal{I}, \mathcal{E}, \tau)$ to denote a table, where we assume that the underlying alphabet is denoted by Σ and the underlying set of strings is denoted by A.

The map τ can be partial. It is of course, possible to allow τ to be a relation, but this generality is unnecessary in the majority of cases.

We now return to the discussion of prefix freeness. Although index sets such as $M = \{Assigns \cdot A1, Assigns \cdot A2, Assigns \cdot A3, Grade\}$ are prefix free, we can express them as a disjoint union of more than one index set. For example, we can partition M into M_1 and M_2, where $M_1 = \{Assigns \cdot A1, Assigns \cdot A2, Assigns \cdot A3\}$ and $M_2 = \{Grade\}$. Note that M_1 cannot be further partitioned without destroying its hierarchical nature. We can capture the partitioning of a prefix-free set as follows. First, we define a function $first$ that extracts the first A-string of a non-null dotted string. For a dotted string x, define $first(x)$ to be undefined if x is the null dotted string; otherwise, it is u, where $u \in A$ and $x = u \cdot v$, for some dotted string v. We can extend $first$ to apply to dotted-string sets as follows: For a dotted-string set Y, $first(Y) = \{u : u \in A$ and $u \cdot v \in Y$, for some dotted string $v\}$. For example, $first(Assigns \cdot A2) = Assigns$. A dotted-string set X is **prime** if all dotted strings in X begin with the same string. In other words, X is prefix free and $\#first(X) = 1$.

Given a prefix-free set X, we can partition it into prime subsets in a unique way, if the prime subsets satisfy an additional condition. A subset Y of a dotted-string set X is a **maximal prime set with respect to X** if all the dotted strings that are in X but are not in Y begin with a different string from the one in $first(Y)$; that is, $first(Y) \cap first(X - Y) = \emptyset$. For example, M_1 and M_2 are maximal with respect to M, but M_1 is not maximal with respect to $M \cup \{Assigns \cdot A4\}$. We obtain the following characterization of partitionability.

Proposition 3. *Let X be a dotted-string set. Then, X can be partitioned into a finite number of prime sets, maximal with respect to X, if and only if X is prefix free. Moreover, this partition is unique.*

In practice, we often use index sets that are not prime; for example, the index set Marks of Table 2 is one such example. Usually, however, we prefer to

Table 2. The average marks for 1991–1992.

	Assignments			Examinations		Grade
	Ass1	Ass2	Ass3	Midterm	Final	
1991						
Winter	85	80	**75**	60	75	75
Spring	80	65	**75**	60	70	70
Fall	80	85	**75**	55	80	75
1992						
Winter	85	80	70	70	75	75
Spring	80	80	70	70	75	75
Fall	75	70	65	60	80	70

premultiply all dotted strings in the index set with one string to ensure that the index set is prime. For example, we can use Marks itself as such a string to obtain $Marks \cdot Assignments \cdot A1$, and so on. This transformation is similar to that used in relational databases when we introduce a universal relation or in an object-oriented environment when we introduce a superclass of all classes. If we do not modify a nonprime index set in this way, then we may not only partition the index set, but also we may partition the corresponding table. For example, we can partition Table 2 into three tables corresponding to the three prime sets obtained from Marks; see Tables 3, 4, and 5.

Prefix-free sets of strings are well known, they are used to define prefix codes. Thus, we can view index sets as codes over an alphabet A. It is well known that prefix codes define labeled trees whose root-to-frontier paths spell out the codewords.

We now introduce a number of useful notions for dotted-string sets. A **common dotted prefix** w of a set X of dotted strings satisfies the condition: *For all dotted strings x in X, $x = w \cdot y$, for some dotted string y.*

Table 3. The average assignment marks for 1991–1992.

	Assignments		
	Ass1	Ass2	Ass3
1991			
Winter	85	80	75
Spring	80	65	75
Fall	80	85	75
1992			
Winter	85	80	70
Spring	80	80	70
Fall	75	70	65

Table 4. The average examination marks for 1991–1992.

	Examinations	
	Midterm	Final
1991		
Winter	60	75
Spring	60	70
Fall	55	80
1992		
Winter	70	75
Spring	70	75
Fall	60	80

Table 5. The average grades for 1991–1992.

	Grade
1991	
Winter	75
Spring	70
Fall	75
1992	
Winter	75
Spring	75
Fall	70

The **dotted length** $\|x\|$ of a dotted string x is 0, if $x = \Lambda$, and is $\|y\| + 1$, otherwise, where $x = y \cdot z$ and $z \in A$. If two dotted strings u and v are common dotted prefixes of a dotted-string set X and $u \neq v$, then either $\|u\| < \|v\|$ or $\|v\| < \|u\|$. Thus, we have the notion of a **longest common dotted prefix** of a set X of dotted strings.

Given two dotted-string sets X and Y, their **dotted product** $X \cdot Y$ is the dotted-string set $\{x \cdot y : x \in X \text{ and } y \in Y\}$. Corresponding to product we have quotient, which comes in two varieties. Given two dotted-string sets X and Y, we can divide Y on the left or on the right with X. We define the **left quotient** $X \backslash Y$ to be the set $\{w : x \in X \text{ and } x \cdot w \in Y\}$ of dotted strings. We define the **right quotient** Y/X to be the set $\{w : x \in X \text{ and } w \cdot x \in Y\}$ of dotted strings.

4   Dotted-string Operations

An effective tabular editor must provide operations that change index sets as well as operations that act on entries and labels. The reason is simple. A user may wish to change the structure of an index set by: adding new labels and indices, removing labels and indices, or modifying indices. These index-set operations involve the addition, removal, and rearrangement of entries in a displayed table. As index sets can have a rich structure, such operations are crucial during tabular design when index sets are more fluid that they will be once the design is frozen (if that ever happens).

Within the dotted-string model, we should have dotted-string set operations that give appropriate operations for index sets. Thus, we are interested in what are the primitive and meaningful operations on index sets that would form the basis of tabular editing operations. We identify two simple operations: adding and removing an index string from an index set. As we shall demonstrate we can specify the semantics of other useful index-set operations in terms of these two.

Addition: $[X' = X + x$ and $X + Y]$. We want to be able to add index strings to an index set, essentially, to form $X \cup \{x\}$, for an index set X and a dotted string x. The set-theoretic union does not always preserve prefix freeness however, so we have to define addition carefully. For an index set X and an index string x, X' is defined as follows:

1. If x is a dotted prefix of some dotted string in X, then $X' = X$.
2. If there is some dotted string $y \neq x$ in X such that y is a dotted prefix of x, then $X' = (X - \{y\}) \cup \{x\}$. Note that there can be at most one such string y in X.
3. Otherwise, $X' = X \cup \{x\}$ and $\#X' = \#X + 1$.

We generalize Addition to allow the second operand to also be an index set. In this case, $X' = X + Y$, where X and Y are both index sets, is defined to be: X, if $Y = \emptyset$; otherwise, it is $(X + y) + (Y - \{y\})$, where $y \in Y$.

Removal: $[X' = X - x$ and $X - Y]$. If we remove a dotted string from an index set, we still have a prefix-free set and an index set. Thus, $X - \{x\}$ is well defined. We define a more general notion of removal, however, that is more appropriate and useful. It removes any dotted string from X that has x as a dotted prefix. It corresponds to the set-theoretic difference when $x \in X$ since, in this case, x is the only dotted string in X having x as a dotted prefix. We define X' as follows: $X' = \{y : y \in X$ and x is a not a dotted prefix of $y\}$. We generalize Removal to allow the second operand to also be a dotted-string set. In this case, $X' = X - Y$, where X is an index set and Y is a dotted-string set, is defined to be: X, if $Y = \emptyset$; otherwise, it is $(X - y) - (Y - \{y\})$, where $y \in Y$. Observe that although Y need not be an index set, the result $X - Y$ is still an index set.

5   Edit Operations

We demonstrate the effectiveness of the conceptual model by showing how we can apply it to specify the semantics of some example edit operations for tables. One initial comment. We define an **empty table** $(\mathcal{I}, \mathcal{E}, \tau)$ to satisfy the conditions: $\mathcal{I} = \emptyset$, $\mathcal{E}$ to be any set of values, and $\tau(())$ to be undefined. We define an **empty category** to be the set $\{\varLambda\}$, rather than the set $\emptyset$ to ensure that the domain of τ is nonempty. We can add an empty category to a table to increase its dimension, yet not increase its size! We model or represent categories with dotted-string sets and, in addition, we use the concept of a **subcategory**; for example, $Examinations$ is a subcategory of $Marks$. We define a subcategory formally using dotted strings. For a dotted-string set X that represents a category C, a dotted-string set Y represents a subcategory S of C if and only if there is a dotted string u such that $\{u\}\backslash X = Y$.

Add-Subcategory: We want to add a category S as a subcategory in a category C of a table $T = (\mathcal{I}, \mathcal{E}, \tau)$. We have to specify where it should be inserted; that is, we have to provide a dotted string x that is a dotted prefix of some of the dotted strings in C. For example, we want to add a new category Special as a subcategory of Term, where $Special \cdot June$ and $Special \cdot July$ correspond to two extremely short special terms. Thus, we should obtain the new indices $Term \cdot Special \cdot June$ and $Term \cdot Special \cdot July$.
Now, Add-Subcategory(S,C,x,T) is defined by: $T' = (\mathcal{I}', \mathcal{E}, \tau')$, where $\mathcal{I}' = (\mathcal{I} - \{C\}) \cup C'$ and τ' is identical to τ over their common domain and is undefined for the new domain values. C' is modeled by an index set; thus, we obtain: If $\{x\}\backslash C \neq \emptyset$ (there are indices with x as a dotted prefix), then

$$C' = C + (\{x\} \cdot S);$$

otherwise, the operation is undefined.

Remove-Subcategory: We want to remove a subcategory S in a category C of a table $T = (\mathcal{I}, \mathcal{E}, \tau)$. We have to specify from where S should be deleted; that is, we have to provide a dotted string x that is a dotted prefix of some of the dotted strings in C. For example, we want to delete the subcategory $Special = \{Special \cdot June, Special \cdot July\}$ from the category Term' used in the previous definition.
Now, Remove-Subcategory(S,C,x,T) is defined by: $T' = (\mathcal{I}', \mathcal{E}, \tau')$, where $\mathcal{I}' = (\mathcal{I} - \{C\}) \cup C'$ and τ' is identical to τ over their common domain. C'

A Conceptual Model for Tables 19

is modeled by an index set; thus, we obtain: If $\{x\}\backslash C \neq \emptyset$ (there are indices with x as a dotted prefix), then

$$C' = C - (\{x\} \cdot S);$$

otherwise, the operation is undefined. Now, C' may be the empty set, in which case we redefine it to be $\{\Lambda\}$ for consistency.

Move-Subcategory: We want to move a subcategory S of a category C within C. We specify S with a dotted string s and its new position with a dotted string t. For example, we want to move the subcategory $A3$ of $Marks$ to be a subcategory of $Examinations$ as a first step in renaming $A3$ as $Quiz$ and treating it as an examination. It is crucial that s is not a dotted prefix of t, although the converse is acceptable.

Now, Move-Subcategory(S,C,s,t,T) is defined by: $T' = (\mathcal{I}', \mathcal{E}, \tau')$, where $\mathcal{I}' = (\mathcal{I} - \{C\}) \cup C'$ and τ' is identical to τ over their common domain. We have to specify the value of τ over its new domain values. We may assume that C is the first category in the domain of τ, as it is an unordered product of $\mathcal{I}$. Now, the only change for the values of τ are that a first index of the form $s \cdot z$, where $z \in S$, no longer occurs. It has been replaced in τ' by an index of the form $t \cdot z$. Thus, for all $z \in S$, we define $\tau'(t \cdot z, i_2, \ldots, i_d) = \tau(s \cdot z, I_2, \ldots, i_d)$.

As C' is modeled by an index set, we obtain: If $\{s\}\backslash C \neq \emptyset$ (there are indices with s as a dotted prefix), $\{t\}\backslash C \neq \emptyset$ (there are indices with t as a dotted prefix), and $\{s\}\backslash\{t\} = \emptyset$ (s is not a dotted prefix of t), then

$$C' = (C - (\{s\} \cdot S)) + (\{t\} \cdot S);$$

otherwise, the operation is undefined.

Combine-Categories: We want to combine two categories C and D of a table $T = (\mathcal{I}, \mathcal{E}, \tau)$ into one new category. The operation does not change the size of the table, but it changes its dimension. Normally, we want to remove any common prefix from the indices in D. For example, we can combine the categories $Year = \{Yr \cdot 91, Yr \cdot 92\}$ and $Term = \{Term \cdot W, Term \cdot Sp, Term \cdot F\}$ to give a new category

$$Year@Term = \{Yr{\cdot}91{\cdot}W, Yr{\cdot}91{\cdot}Sp, Yr{\cdot}91{\cdot}F, Yr{\cdot}92{\cdot}W, Yr{\cdot}92{\cdot}Sp, Yr{\cdot}92{\cdot}F\},$$

where we have used obvious abbreviations and @ is a new symbol. Note that we have removed the prefix $Term$ from the index strings in Term.

Combine-Categories(C,D,x,T) is defined by: $T' = (\mathcal{I}', \mathcal{E}, \tau')$, where $\mathcal{I}' = (\mathcal{I} - \{C\} - \{D\}) \cup C'$.

Clearly, we want to model this operation by a product of index sets; If $D = \{x\} \cdot (\{x\}\backslash D)$ (x is a common prefix of the index strings in D), then we define $C' = C \cdot (\{x\}\backslash D)$

We can assume that categories C and D occur as the first two categories in $\mathcal{I}$ and that C' occurs as the first category in $\mathcal{I}'$. Thus, τ' is defined by: $\tau'(c \cdot (x\backslash d), i_3, \ldots, i_d) = \tau(c, d, i_3, \ldots, i_d)$.

Using this operation we can convert any d-dimensional table into a one-dimensional one. Presentationally, such a table has only either a box head or a stub.

6 Expressiveness of the Conceptual Model

We have made the simplying assumption that we do not model footnotes in the conceptual model. Clearly, footnotes play an important role in tables. For example, in the book *Human Activity and Environment* [1], 148 of the 172 tables have footnotes. The conceptual model does not capture all tables even when we ignore footnotes but in our view it is sufficiently powerful to be useful—it provides at a "70 percent solution" to use one of guidelines of software engineers. Footnotes can, however, be included but they are passed without interpretation to the user's text formatter. This approach is viable since the footnotes themselves do not appear within tables, they are placed outside the tables. Only the associated footnote marks are included in the tables.

The model can be used to specify only tables that have a structure that corresponds to the conceptual model. Some tables, however, are a combination of several tables. Some do not distinguish between a label and an entry and some do not even have a rectangular frame. For example, Table 6 is a combination of three tables. There are three index sets: X, Y, and *Type of calculations* (the index set in the stub head) in this table. The first subtable, whose entries are associated with the categories X and *Type of calculations*, has been placed in the boxhead. The second subtable, whose entries are associated with the index sets Y and *Type of calculations*, has been placed in the stub. The third subtable, whose entries are associated with index sets X and Y, has been placed in the body.

We examined tables in books from various sources, including statistics, sociology, science, and business. The results of the experiment reveal that the conceptual model can be used to specify 56 percent of the tables if we consider footnotes or 97 percent of the tables if we ignore footnotes. From this experiment, we see that the majority of the tables in traditional printed documents can be specified with our conceptual model.

7 Last Words

We have left a number of issues unresolved, both implications for other tabular manipulations, such as display, and completeness of the edit operations. Wang [21], and Wang and Wood [23] have developed a style language for tables that allows a user to specify global, and local styles for tables with respect to a table's conceptual structure, topological structure, and presentational structure. Although this work is based on an earlier abstract model for tables, there is little difficulty in adapting it for the conceptual model we have described.

All models have their up sides and down sides. On the up side, the conceptual model captures the hierarchical structure of index sets and their unordered combination—key properties in our opinion. The downside is that the frugality of the model moves the specification of orderings outside the model, although the user of a tabular system should be unaware of this fact. We chose this option since we wanted to separate structure from display; it is sufficient that we can hang display issues on top of the conceptual model.

Lastly, a number of readers of the draft of this paper commented that there is some overlap in ideas with the work on OLAP (On-Line Analytical Processing), a key high-level notion in data mining and knowledge discovery [8, 9, 11]. OLAP is especially concerned with the processing of very large collections of data that have high dimensionality. Although the viewpoint and concern of OLAP is different, there are indeed similarities in the models. We will address their similarities and differences in the full version of this paper.

References

1. *Human Activity and the Environment—A Statistical Compendium.* Statistics Canada, 1986.
2. M.P. Barnett. *Computer Typesetting: Experiments and Prospects.* MIT Press, 1965.
3. R.J. Beach. *Setting Tables and Illustrations with Style.* PhD thesis, Dept. of Computer Science, University of Waterloo, Waterloo, Ontario, Canada, May 1985. Also issued as Technical Report CSL-85-3, Xerox Palo Alto Research Center, Palo Alto, CA.
4. J.L. Bentley. *More Programming Pearls: Confessions of a Coder.* Addison-Wesley, Reading, MA, 1988. Chapter 9 is an excellent apologia for little languages.
5. T.J. Biggerstaff, D.M. Endres, and I.R. Forman. TABLE: Object oriented editing of complex structures. In *Proceeding of the 7th International Conference on Software Engineering*, pages 334–345, 1984.
6. F.P. Brooks. *The Mythical Man-Month: Essays in Software Engineering.* Addison-Wesley, Reading, MA, second edition, 1975. Reprinted with corrections, January 1982.
7. J.P. Cameron. A cognitive model for tabular editing. Technical Report OSU-CISRC-6/89-TR 26, The Ohio State University, Columbus, OH, June 1989.
8. S. Chaudhuri and U. Dayal. An overview of data warehousing and OLAP technology. *ACM SIGMOD Record*, 26(2):65–74, 1997.
9. E.F. Codd, S.B. Codd, and C.T. Shelley. Providing OLAP (On-line Analytical Processing to User-Analysts. Technical report, Codd & Date, Inc., 1993.
10. R. Furuta. *An Integrated but not Exact-Representation, Editor/Formatter.* PhD thesis, Dept. of Computer Science, University of Washington, Seattle, WA, September 1986. Also issued as Technical Report 86-09-08, University of Washington.
11. C.-T. Ho, R. Agrawal, N. Megiddo, and R. Srikant. Range queries in OLAP data cubes. *ACM SIGMOD Record*, 26(2):73–78, 1997.
12. International Organization for Standardization. *ISO 8879, Information processing — Text and office systems — Standard Generalized Markup Language(SGML)*, October 1986.
13. International Organization for Standardization and International Electrotechnical Commission. *ISO/IEC TR 9573:1988(E), Information processing — SGML Support Facilities — Techniques for Using SGML*, 1988.
14. International Organization for Standardization and International Electrotechnical Commission. *ISO/IEC TR 9573-11:1992(E), Information processing — SGML Support Facilities — Techniques for Using SGML*, 1992.
15. L. Lamport. *LaTeX: A Document Preparation System.* Addison-Wesley, Reading, MA, 1985.

16. M.E. Lesk. Tbl—a program to format tables. In *UNIX Programmer's Manual*, volume 2A. Bell Telephone Laboratories, Murray Hill, NJ, 7th edition, January 1979.

17. V. Quint and I. Vatton. Grif: An interactive system for structured document manipulation. In *Text Processing and Document Manipulation, Proceedings of the International Conference*, pages 200–312, Cambridge, UK, 1986. Cambridge University Press.

18. D.R. Raymond. *Partial Order Databases*. PhD thesis, Department of Computer Science, University of Waterloo, Waterloo, Ontario, Canada, 1996.

19. C. Vanoirbeek. *Une Modelisation de Documents pour le Formatage*. PhD thesis, Departement d'Informatique, École Polytechnique Fédérale de Lausanne, Lausanne, Switzerland, 1988.

20. C. Vanoirbeek. Formatting structured tables. In C. Vanoirbeek & G. Coray, editor, *EP92 (Proceedings of Electronic Publishing, 1992)*, pages 291–309, Cambridge, UK, 1992. Cambridge University Press.

21. X. Wang. *Tabular Abstraction, Editing and Formatting*. PhD thesis, Department of Computer Science, University of Waterloo, Waterloo, Ontario, Canada, 1996. Available as Research Report CS-96-09, Department of Computer Science, University of Waterloo.

22. X. Wang and D. Wood. An abstract model for tables. TUGBOAT, *The Communications of the TEX Users Group*, 14(3):231–237, October 1993.

23. X. Wang and D. Wood. Xtable—a tabular editor and formatter. *Electronic Publishing: Origination, Dissemination and Design*, 8:167–179, 1995. Special issue for papers that appeared in Electronic Publishing '96.

Table 6. Correlation table — wheat and flour prices by months, 1914–1933.

X

class interval	mid-point	deviation d	frequency f	fd	fd²	.40-.59	.60-.79	.80-.99	1.00-1.19	1.20-1.39	1.40-1.59	1.60-1.79	1.80-1.99	2.00-2.19	2.20-2.39	2.40-2.59	2.60-2.79	2.80-2.99	Total	f(dxdy)
	mid-point					5	7	9	11	13	15	17	19	21	23	25	27	29		
		deviation d				0	1	2	3	4	5	6	7	8	9	10	11	12		
			frequency f			20	6	25	37	52	24	15	15	13	18	6	5	4	240	
				fd		0	6	50	111	208	120	90	105	104	162	60	55	48	1119	
					fd²	0	6	100	333	832	600	540	735	832	1458	600	605	576	7217	
15.00-15.99	15.5	12	1	12	144													1	1	144
14.00-14.99	14.5	11	5	55	605											1	2	2	5	616
13.00-13.99	13.5	10	5	50	500										1	2	1	1	5	520
12.00-12.99	12.5	9	10	90	810										6	2	2		10	864
11.00-11.99	11.5	8	5	40	320									1	3	1			5	360
10.00-10.99	10.5	7	14	98	686									6	8				14	840
9.00-9.99	9.5	6	17	102	612						1	1	10	5					17	726
8.00-8.99	8.5	5	28	140	700					4	8	11	4	1					28	790
7.00-7.99	7.5	4	46	184	736			2	7	22	12	3							46	764
6.00-6.99	6.5	3	54	162	486			5	20	25	3		1						54	576
5.00-5.99	5.5	2	16	32	64		1	4	10	1									16	86
4.00-4.99	4.5	1	34	34	34	15	5	14											34	33
3.00-3.99	3.5	0	5	0	0	5													5	0
Total			240	999	5697															6319

Y

X= Wheat price per bushel in dollars; Y= Flour price per barrel in dollars.

Analysis of Document Structures
for Element Type Classification

Helena Ahonen[1], Barbara Heikkinen[2], Oskari Heinonen[2],
Jani Jaakkola[2], and Mika Klemettinen[2] *

[1] University of Tübingen, Wilhelm-Schickard-Institut für Informatik,
Sand 13, D-72076 Tübingen, Germany
[2] University of Helsinki, Department of Computer Science,
P.O. Box 26 (Teollisuuskatu 23), FIN–00014 University of Helsinki, Finland
Phone: +358 9 70 851, Fax: +358 9 7084 4441

Abstract. As more and more digital documents become available for
the public use from different sources, also the needs of the users increase. Seamless integration of heterogenous collections, e.g., a possibil-
ity to query and format documents in a uniform way, is one of these
needs. Processing of documents is greatly enhanced if the structure of
documents is explicitly represented by some standard (SGML, XML,
HTML). Hence, the problem of integrating heterogenous structures has
to be taken into consideration.
We address this problem by introducing a classification method that
acquires knowledge from document instances and their document type
definitions, and uses this knowledge to attach a generic class to each
SGML element type. The classification retains the tree hierarchy of elements. Although the structure is simplified, enough distinctions remain
to facilitate versatile further processing, e.g., formatting. The class of an
element type can be stored in the document type definition and, using
the architectural form feature of SGML, the documents can be processed
as virtual documents obeying a pre-defined generic DTD.
The specific usages of the classification, in addition to formatting and
querying, include assembly of new documents from existing document
fragments and automatic generation of style sheet templates for original document type definitions. We have implemented the classification
method and experimented with several document types.

1 Introduction

Standard Generalized Markup Language (SGML) [7] has speeded up the document processing by giving a way to structure documents and to guide their
processing in a standardized way. As the SGML community expands, more and
more documents become available for users. However, when moving from pro-
prietary document collections to widely-available digital collections, we imme-
diately face the problem of heterogeneous document structures. For instance,

---

* Authors' e-mail addresses: {Helena.Ahonen, Barbara.Heikkinen, Oskari.Heinonen,
Jani.Jaakkola, Mika.Klemettinen}@cs.Helsinki.FI.

we cannot assume anymore that the user knows how the documents are structured and what are the exact names of the elements. Moreover, the availability of digital collections creates new possibilities and desires to combine fragments of documents in order to construct new documents.

To address the problem of heterogeneous structures we need tools for analyzing SGML documents and for extracting some essential information that enable uniform processing of them. Our approach is to classify the elements in the documents to several generic classes. Classification is based on the document instances and the document type definitions (DTD): we analyze the nesting of elements within each other, lengths of the elements, and the existence of children. Whereas, no inferring is based on the names of the elements. The process simplifies the structure but retains the tree skeleton. As original element names can be stored as attributes, the detailed structure can be recalled later if necessary.

Several usages for the classification can be found. Probably the most common need to process documents is to print them. If we have a set of documents from different sources and we just desire to obtain some readable format, we can classify the documents in order to find a generic class for each element type present, and then format the documents using a style sheet for the generic DTD. An even more advanced application is constructing automatic generators of style sheets for different DTDs. If we know the generic classes for element types, we can, using the semantics of the classes, generate a style sheet template, which can then be tuned by the user, if necessary.

Classification can also be used to aid document transformations. Instead of writing specific translators between all the document types, we need to write them only between each type and the generic type, if we first transform the elements to generic elements. Clearly, we reduce the complexity of the structures each time we apply the transformations.

If the elements are classified, the user can query or browse the documents based on the structure, even if he/she does not know the original structure. For instance, our method can recognize most of the title elements as titles, and hence the query can be directed to the titles only. As the original DTDs are also available, the user can also study a DTD with the help of the classes. For instance, a query "select all elements where class=String" can be stated. This kind of queries might be an invaluable tool also for a system analyst that needs to get an overview of the collection and both the structure and semantics of the documents.

As already mentioned, assembly of new documents using fragments from different sources is an emerging application in the document management. In an on-going research and development project called Structured and Intelligent Documents (SID) [3] we study *document assembly* in its different aspects.

Assembly is an interactive process within which an author or editor uses various tools to find appropriate sources and to configure the intended document. The process consists of two parts: 1) finding the interesting document fragments and 2) constructing a coherent document from these fragments. For an exposition of our assembly system, see [2]. The classification enables easier controlling of transformations in forming a composite document, which furthermore should be a valid SGML document.

Somewhat related to our approach is the research done on semi-structured data management [1, 5, 11]. In that area, however, the emphasis on the database issues and the goal to be able to handle also only implicitly structured non-SGML documents make the research problems different. Although some work [6, 10] includes classification of text elements, their approaches differ from ours and cannot be used to solve all the problems we intend to solve.

The rest of this paper is organized as follows. Section 2 describes the structural analysis process, while Section 3 explains in detail how the classification algorithm recognizes elements and attaches classes to them. In Section 4 a meta-DTD which controls all the resulting documents is introduced. Some results of the experiments are discussed in Section 5, and Section 6 is a short conclusion.

2   Classification of Element Types

SGML is a metalanguage for defining document structures. The logical structural parts, *elements*, of an SGML document are marked up by start and end *tags*. The set of element names and the permitted structures of the elements are given in the *document type definition* (DTD) that is essentially a context-free grammar, in which the right-hand sides of the rules are regular expressions. A DTD can be used to facilitate structured queries and various transformations needed, e.g., to produce multiple output formats. SGML representation defines only the syntax of the structures: any semantics, e.g., how the elements should be formatted for printing, has to be attached by some application. The aim of the element type classification presented in this paper is to map every element type of an SGML document to some generic element class with well-known semantics, particularly in order to facilitate processing of heterogeneous or partially unknown document collections.

For the classification of element types in the given document collection, we introduce a novel algorithm, which is based on average element lengths and the structural information of the initial document. The classification process constitutes of three main phases (see Figure 1):

1. Scanning through the original documents and calculating average lengths and sizes for element types and their substructures.
2. Pre-classification of the element types.
3. Final classification of the element types.

In the first phase, all the documents are traversed once to collect the set of element names, and for each element, the set of elements it contains as well as the average length of its content. Thereafter, in the second and third phases, each element type is mapped to some generic element class like section (*Section*), paragraph container (*ParaCont*), paragraph (*Para*), string container (*StrCont*), or string (*String*). Pre-classification is done bottom-up in the element type tree, whereas final classification proceeds from root to leaves. There is a table of all the different element classes in Appendix A.

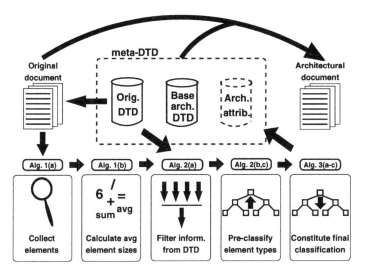

Fig. 1. The classification process from the original document and DTD to architectural document with our algorithm. The dotted line represents objects that are created during the process.

Example 1. This simple example shows an excerpt of an original tagged document [4] and an architectural document, i.e., a classified document, using generic elements. The original document uses the Book DTD of ISO 12083. The DTD for the architectural document and the full element type mapping for that particular book can be found in Section 4. Longer examples can be found in Appendices B and C.

Original Document:[1]

```
<SECTION><NO>1</NO>
  ...
  <P>Alice Freeman needed cash desperately. She was in debt. ...
    She described her experience at Lake Geneva in a letter to her friend
    Lucy Andrews.
    <BQ><P>The days have been very trying to me for...</P></BQ>
    She went on to describe her work:
    <BQ><P>. . . it isn't so very hard or wearing. ...</P></BQ>
    ...
  </P>
```

Architectural Document:

```
<SECTION><TITLE>1</TITLE>
  ...
  <PARA>Alice Freeman needed cash desperately. She was in debt. ...
    She described her experience at Lake Geneva in a letter to her friend
    Lucy Andrews.
    <PARACONT><PARA>The days have been very trying to me for...</PARA></PARACONT>
    She went on to describe her work:
    <PARACONT><PARA>. . . it isn't so very hard or wearing. ...</PARA></PARACONT>
    ...
  </PARA>
```

---

[1] Element type *BQ* stands for blockquotes, and *P* for paragraphs.

3   Algorithms

In the following sections, we present the detailed algorithm to accomplish the element type classification. The phases of the classification process are illustrated in Figure 1.

3.1   Calculating Average Lengths and Sizes

Algorithm 1(a) Algorithm 1(a) gathers and outputs statistics of each node of the SGML instance tree: the name of the element, a list of the names of the children, the length of text data (*#PCDATA*) of the element, and the length of text data in the subtree of the element. The element is considered to be the root of its subtree, i.e., text data of the element is also included in the subtree. The query of Algorithm 1(a) is performed to each document instance of a document class.

We have used different kinds of documents and document collections as the test data for our algorithm. In our experiments, the size of the query result was usually between one third and half of the size of the original document instances. For instance, one of our test document classes contains 3 textbooks, altogether 2.7 MB. In this case the size of the query result was 0.9 MB of text data. We have also access to a collection of approximately 50,000 Finnish statutes, altogether hundreds of megabytes of text. We used a sample of 24.5 MB, and the size of the query result was 14.5 MB. If the average element length is small, then the result size is closer to the original size. For example, a collection of poems by Shakespeare, originally 7.5 MB, produced 7.1 MB of query results.

Algorithm 1(a):

(1)   **foreach** element *e* in SGML tree of source document **do**
(2)   output name of element *e.name*:
(3)   output names of children *e.children*;
(4)   output length of text data in element *e.text*;
(5)   output length of text data in subtree of element *e.subtree*;

$\square$

Algorithm 1(b) Algorithm 1(b) establishes the necessary data structures and counts average information of the different element types of the input, which is the output of Algorithm 1(a). For each element instance, the collected information is processed (row 2). If a new element type is encountered (row 3), the element name is inserted to *elemList*, which is a list of different element types (row 4), and the data structures of the element type are initialized (rows 5–10). Then the counter for element instances is updated (row 11), the names of new children are inserted to *childList* (rows 12–14), and the counter for the text length of the element and its subtree is updated (rows 15–16). After processing the input, average text-length information is computed for each different element type (rows 17–19).

Algorithm 1(b):

(1) $elemList := \emptyset$;
(2)   **foreach** element e in input **do**
(3)   **if** $(e.name \notin elemList)$ **then**
(4)   push$(elemList,\ e.name)$;
(5) $count_{e.name} := 0$;
(6) $childList_{e.name} := \emptyset$;
(7) $text_{e.name} := 0$;
(8) $subtree_{e.name} := 0$;
(9) $candClasses_{e.name} := \emptyset$;
(10) $finalClass_{e.name} := \emptyset$;
(11) $count_{e.name} := count_{e.name} + 1$;
(12)   **foreach** child $c \in e.children$ **do**
(13)   **if** $(c \notin childList_{e.name})$ **then**
(14)   push$(childList_{e.name},\ c)$;
(15) $text_{e.name} := text_{e.name} + e.text$;
(16) $subtree_{e.name} := subtree_{e.name} + e.subtree$;
(17)   **foreach** element type $elem \in elemList$ **do**
(18) $avgText_{elem} := text_{elem} / count_{elem}$;
(19) $avgSubtree_{elem} := subtree_{elem} / count_{elem}$;

□

3.2   Pre-classification of the Element Types

Algorithm 2(a) Information from the DTD is filtered in Algorithm 2(a). When an element type is classified, it is removed from the *elemList*. Therefore, the original *elemList* has to be copied to *origList* (row 1). In the DTD, the element type can be defined to be *EMPTY* (row 3). In such case, *Empty* is inserted to $candClasses_{e.name}$, the set of candidate classes of the element type (row 4). Moreover, if an element type has a *NOTATION* attribute informing a graphics format, e.g., GIF, TIFF, or WMF, defined in the DTD (row 6), then the element type is defined to be of class *Fig* (row 7). The function *ClassifyElement* inserts the class to $candClasses_{e.name}$ and removes the element type from *elemList* (Algorithm 2(c), rows 1–3). If the type of an attribute is *IDREF* (one reference) or *IDREFS* (a list of references) and the element type is empty, the element type is defined to be of class *Link* (rows 8–10). If the referencing element type has got a text length shorter than *MAXSTR* (60 characters), the resulting class is *Ref* (row 11).

Algorithm 2(a):

(1) $origList := elemList$;
(2)   **foreach** element type $elem \in elemList$ **do**
(3)   **if** $(elem$ is defined EMPTY$)$ **then**
(4) $candClasses_{elem} := $ "Empty";
(5)   **foreach** element type $elem \in elemList$ **do**
(6)   **if** $(elem$ has a graphics NOTATION attribute$)$ **then**

(7)   ClassifyElement($elem$, "Fig");
(8)   **elsif** ($avgText_{elem} \leq MAXSTR \wedge elem$ has an IDREF attribute) **then**
(9)   **if** ($candClasses_{elem} =$ "Empty") **then**
(10)   ClassifyElement($elem$, "Link");
(11)   **else** ClassifyElement($elem$, "Ref");

□

Algorithm 2(b–c) The element type tree is traversed from leaves to root in Algorithm 2(b). First the leaf-level element types are processed (Step 1, rows 1–6). The element type is a leaf node, if it does not have any children, i.e., the *childList* of an element type is empty (row 2). Then, if the element type does not have any text content, it is classified as *Empty* (rows 3–4), and if the text length is smaller than a threshold for strings ($MAXSTR$), it is classified as *String* (rows 5–6). In practice, a good threshold size for $MAXSTR$ has been 60 characters.

The middle-level element types are classified in Step 2 (rows 7–13). As long as new element types are found, we iterate the following (row 7). If all the children of the element type are classified (row 9), we may proceed. If the element type does not have any text content (row 10), it is of container type (function *StrLevel*; Algorithm 2(c), row 4): If at least one child contains graphics, the element type is classified as *FigCont*, i.e., figure container (rows 5–6). If some children are of type *StrCont* or *StrGrp*, the class of the element type will be *StrGrp*, i.e., string group (rows 7–8). Otherwise, the class will be *StrCont*, i.e., string container. On the other hand, if the element type has got a text length smaller than $MAXSTR$, it is not a container, but of class *String* (rows 12–13).

Step 3 (rows 14–27) is for the upper levels of the element type tree. As long as new element types are found, the following iteration will be executed (row 14). If the average text length is greater than $MINSECT$, the element type is classified as *Section* (rows 16–17), although *Sections* are mainly identified in the final classification phase of Algorithm 3(a–c). It is unlikely that this kind of element types occur if the document markup is properly designed. We have used a threshold value of 1,000 characters. If the text length is between string and section thresholds, the element class is set to *Para* meaning a paragraph component (rows 18–19). Finally, the rest of the element types directly containing text are classified as *Strings*.

Because of the previous conditions the text length is now 0 (rows 22–). Hence, if the element type contains *Paras*, it is classified as a container *ParaCont* (rows 22–23). Now we take a tighter condition assuming that all the children must be classified (row 24). If the container does not have *Paras* and has at least one *ParaCont* or *ParaGrp*, it is of class *ParaGrp* (rows 25–26). The difference between *ParaCont* and *ParaGrp* is that the container has *Paras* as children. Because of this distinction we can have a richer resulting tree structure. The same holds with *StrConts* and *StrGrps*. Finally the function *StrLevel* is called again in order to define string-level containers in the upper parts of the tree (e.g., a title group of a book).

Algorithm 2(b):

```
(1)    foreach element type elem ∈ elemList do // Step 1
(2)         if (childList_elem = ∅) then
(3)              if (text_elem = 0) then
(4)                   ClassifyElement(elem, "Empty");
(5)              elsif (avgText_elem ≤ MAXSTR) then
(6)                   ClassifyElement(elem, "String");
(7)    while new candClasses are found do // Step 2
(8)         foreach element type elem ∈ elemList do
(9)              if (∄child | child ∈ childList_elem ∧ candClasses_child = ∅) then
(10)                  if (avgText_elem = 0) then
(11)                       StrLevel(elem);
(12)                  elsif (avgText_elem ≤ MAXSTR) then
(13)                       ClassifyElement(elem, "String");
(14)   while new candClasses are found do // Step 3
(15)        foreach element type elem ∈ elemList do
(16)             if (avgText_elem ≥ MINSECT) then
(17)                  ClassifyElement(elem, "Section");
(18)             elsif (avgText_elem > MAXSTR ∧ avgText_elem < MINSECT) then
(19)                  ClassifyElement(elem, "Para");
(20)             elsif (avgText_elem > 0 ∧ avgText_elem ≤ MAXSTR) then
(21)                  ClassifyElement(elem, "String");
(22)             elsif (∃child | child ∈ childList_elem
                          ∧ "Para" ∈ candClasses_child) then
(23)                  ClassifyElement(elem, "ParaCont");
(24)             elsif (∄child | child ∈ childList_elem ∧ candClasses_child = ∅) then
(25)                  if ((∄child | child ∈ childList_elem ∧ "Para" ∈ candClasses_child)
                          ∧ (∃child | child ∈ childList_elem
                               ∧ ("ParaCont" ∈ candClasses_child
                                    ∨ "ParaGrp" ∈ candClasses_child))) then
(26)                       ClassifyElement(elem, "ParaGrp");
(27)                  else StrLevel(elem);
```

□

Algorithm 2(c):

```
(1)    function ClassifyElement(elem, class)
(2)         candClasses_elem := class;
(3)         remove(elemList, elem);
(4)    function StrLevel(elem)
(5)         if (∃child | child ∈ childList_elem ∧ "Fig" ∈ candClasses_child) then
(6)              ClassifyElement(elem, "FigCont");
(7)         elsif (∃child | child ∈ childList_elem ∧
                     ("StrCont" ∈ candClasses_child ∨ "StrGrp" ∈ candClasses_child)) then
(8)              ClassifyElement(elem, "StrGrp");
(9)         else ClassifyElement(elem, "StrCont");
```

□

3.3   Final Classification

The element type tree is traversed from the root to the leaves in Algorithm 3. The idea is to classify element types containing paragraph containers or paragraph groups as sections, and to finally find the title element types in the structure.

Algorithm 3(a) The first element in the input of Algorithm 1(b) is the root element. Therefore, it can be found in the beginning of the element type list (row 1, Algorithm 3(a)). The root, *VirtDoc*, is inserted to the candidate classes and final classes of the first element type (rows 2 and 5). For the actual classification task, two recursive functions, *traverse* (Algorithm 3(b)) and *traverseFinal* (Algorithm 3(c)), are called (rows 4 and 6). After finding the section structure, title element types are recognized as the first *String* child of a higher level element type (rows 8–9). The rule could be more permissive in order to find more titles. For instance, if the parent element type is *VirtDoc*, *SecGrp* or *Section*, the child might also be of type *StrCont* to be a title.

Algorithm 3(a):

(1) $firstelem := origList.first$; // $origList$ defined in Algorithm 2a
(2) $candClasses_{firstelem} := candClasses_{firstelem} \cup$ "VirtDoc";
(3) $typesOfSecs := \{$"SecGrp", "Section"$\}$;
(4) traverse(" ", $firstelem$, $childList_{firstelem}$, 1);
(5) $finalClass_{firstelem} :=$ "VirtDoc";
(6) traverseFinal(" ", $firstelem$, $childList_{firstelem}$);
(7) **foreach** element type $elem \in origList$ **do** // find the titles
(8)   **if** $(\{finalClass_{elem}\} \setminus \{$"StrGrp", "ParaCont", "ParaGrp",
            "Section", "SecGrp", "VirtDoc"$\} = \emptyset$
         $\land finalClass_{childList_{elem}.first} =$ "String") **then**
(9) $finalClass_{childList_{elem}.first} :=$ "Title";

$\square$

Algorithm 3(b) In Algorithm 3(b) the element type tree is traversed recursively as long as at least one child of the current element type can be classified as *ParaCont* or *ParaGrp*. The rules *child ≠ parent* and *child ≠ grandp* are needed to prevent an endless recursion in the case of recursive element type chains. Here the checking is simplified by considering parents and grandparents only, but in the worst case, a long list of ancestors need to be tested. If an element type of the class *Section* is encountered, the information of the level in the tree is concatenated with the section. This level information is not utilized explicitly in these algorithms, but it could be saved enabling, for example, the recognition of different levels of sections in the document formatting phase.

Algorithm 3(b):

(1)　**function** traverse($grandp$, $parent$, $childList_{parent}$, $level$)
(2)　　　**foreach** $child \in childList_{parent}$ **do**
(3)　　　　**if** (("ParaCont" $\in candClasses_{child}$ ∨ "ParaGrp" $\in candClasses_{child}$)
　　　　　　∧ $child \neq parent \wedge child \neq grandp$) **then**
(4)　　　　　　$candClasses_{child} := candClasses_{child} \cup$ concat("Section", $level$);
(5)　　　　　　$typesOfSecs := typesOfSecs \cup$ concat("Section", $level$);
(6)　　　　　　traverse($parent$, $child$, $childList_{child}$, $level + 1$);

□

Algorithm 3(c) In Algorithm 3(c) a final traverse from root to section elements is made. An element type belongs to the section level if the final class of its parent element type belongs to the section level, at least one of the candidate classes of the child belongs to the section level, and the average text length of the subtree of the child is greater than $MINSECT$ (rows 3–4). If the candidate classes of the child contain a paragraph container, the child is classified to be pure *Section* (rows 4–6). Otherwise the child is a section group, *SecGrp* (rows 7–9). It is useful to identify pure sections which contain the actual textual part from section groups. For instance, if a book structure contains a body, which is a container for chapters but itself does not contain any text, it is reasonable to divide the body to be of class *SecGrp* and the chapter to be of class *Section*. If it appears that the child does not belong to the section level, the final class of the child will be the same as the candidate class first given in Algorithm 2(b) (rows 10–12).

Algorithm 3(c):

(1)　**function** traverseFinal($grandp$, $parent$, $childList_{parent}$)
(2)　　　**foreach** $child \in childList_{parent}$ **do**
(3)　　　　**if** (($finalClass_{parent}$ = "VirtDoc" ∨ $finalClass_{parent} \in typesOfSecs$)
　　　　　　∧ $avgSubtree_{child} > MINSECT$
　　　　　　∧ $child \neq parent \wedge child \neq grandp$) **then**
(4)　　　　　　**if** (($\exists c \mid c \in candClasses_{child} \wedge c \in typesOfSecs$)
　　　　　　　　∧ "ParaCont" $\in candClasses_{child}$) **then**
(5)　　　　　　　　$finalClass_{child} :=$ "Section";
(6)　　　　　　　　traverseFinal($parent$, $child$, $childList_{child}$);
(7)　　　　　　**elsif** (($\exists c \mid c \in candClasses_{child} \wedge c \in typesOfSecs$)
　　　　　　　　∧ "ParaGrp" $\in candClasses_{child}$) **then**
(8)　　　　　　　　$finalClass_{child} :=$ "SecGrp";
(9)　　　　　　　　traverseFinal($parent$, $child$, $childList_{child}$);
(10)　　　　**elsif** ($finalClass_{child} = \emptyset$) **then**
(11)　　　　　　$finalClass_{child} := \{c \mid c \in candClasses_{child}\} \setminus typesOfSecs$;
(12)　　　　　　traverseFinal($parent$, $child$, $childList_{child}$);

□

3.4   Time Complexity of the Algorithms

The query of Algorithm 1(a) can be implemented to run in linear time $\mathcal{O}(n)$, where n is the number of the element nodes in the tree.[2] Consider that the tree is traversed from the leaves to the root. When the step to the upper node is taken, all the necessary information is available in the node and in the children of the node; i.e., each node is traversed only once. Example 2 is one possible TranSID solution to Algorithm 1(a). TranSID [9] is a transformation language, which models documents as tree structures, and allows any part of the document tree to be accessed.

Example 2. TranSID query for Algorithm 1(a).

```
query (source, source.descendants).elements.map(true;
   "<", this.name, ">\n",
   "\tChildren:", this.children.elements.map(true; " ", this.name), "\n",
   "\tText: ", this.children.data.strcat.strlen, "\n",
   "\tSubtree: ", this.descendants.data.strcat.strlen, "\n");
```

The running time of Algorithm 1(b) is $\mathcal{O}(n)$, where n is the number of element nodes in the document tree. The statistics of each of the n nodes is processed once (rows 2–16). The complexity of rows 17–19 is $\mathcal{O}(e)$, where $e \leq n$ is the number of different element types. In practice, the size of n is from thousands up to a few millions of nodes, and the size of e is from dozens up to a few hundred element types.

The time complexity of Algorithms 2 and 3 is in practice $\mathcal{O}(e)$ and in the worst case $\mathcal{O}(e^2)$. It remains marginal when compared to $\mathcal{O}(n)$ of Algorithm 1(a–b), because the size of e is only a small fraction of the size of n. Thus, the time complexity of the whole algorithm is $\mathcal{O}(n)$.

In our experiments, we had a document collection of size 65 MB. The classification procedure (without TranSID queries) took about 10 minutes of real time with an Alpha-based computer running Linux OS. Less than half of a minute was dedicated for Algorithms 2 and 3, while the rest was consumed in Algorithm 1(b) reading the node information and calculating the averages. Algorithms 1(b), 2 and 3 were implemented using Perl.

4   Meta-DTD for the Architectural Document

In this section we show how the classification of element types can be used with the SGML architectural forms facility [8] to create *architectural documents*, or virtual documents. Suppose we want to create a more general or simplified structure for a given document collection; for instance, we may want the DTD to be more permissive. The original documents are transformed into architectural documents by retaining the contents of the documents but mapping the original element types into new ones.[3] Typically, the amount of element types is reduced.

---

[2] We omit the time requirement of parsing the DTD because that is not the problem here. With large documents the size of the DTD is, in practice, negligible compared with the size of the document instances.

[3] It would also be possible to make mappings that alter the document contents, e.g., by ignoring some element types.

When creating the resulting virtual documents, we need the following three components (see also Figure 1):

- original DTD,
- base architecture DTD, and
- architectural form attributes.

Together they form a *meta-DTD* for a specified document collection. To be more precise: From the original DTD we get the initial element type definitions, the base architecture DTD (see Example 3) gives us the target element type definitions, and finally the architectural form attributes provide us the mapping between the initial and the target element types. In our setting, the element type classification produces the mapping, whereas the base architecture DTD is pre-defined using the generic element classes.

Example 3. The base architecture DTD for *VirtDoc* architectural documents.

```
<!ELEMENT VirtDoc    - -  (Empty|Link|Ref|Fig|FigCont|Title|String|StrCont|StrGrp|Formula|
                          Table|Para|ParaCont|ParaGrp|Section|SecGrp)*>

<!ELEMENT SecGrp     - -  (Empty|Link|Ref|Fig|FigCont|Title|String|StrCont|StrGrp|Formula|
                          Table|ParaCont|ParaGrp|Section|SecGrp)*>
<!ELEMENT Section    - -  (Empty|Link|Ref|Fig|FigCont|Title|String|StrCont|StrGrp|Formula|
                          Table|Para|ParaCont|ParaGrp|Section|SecGrp)*>

<!ELEMENT ParaGrp    - -  (Empty|Link|Ref|Fig|FigCont|Title|String|StrCont|StrGrp|Formula|
                          Table|ParaCont|ParaGrp)*>
<!ELEMENT ParaCont   - -  (Empty|Link|Ref|Fig|FigCont|Title|String|StrCont|StrGrp|Formula|
                          Table|Para|ParaCont|ParaGrp)*>
<!ELEMENT Para       - -  ((#PCDATA)|Empty|Link|Ref|Fig|FigCont|String|StrCont|StrGrp|Formula|
                          Table|Para|ParaCont|ParaGrp)*>

<!ELEMENT StrGrp     - -  (Empty|Link|Ref|Fig|FigCont|Title|String|StrCont|StrGrp|Formula|
                          Table)*>
<!ELEMENT StrCont    - -  (Empty|Link|Ref|Fig|FigCont|Title|String|StrCont|Formula)*>
<!ELEMENT String     - -  ((#PCDATA)|Empty|Link|Ref|Fig|FigCont|String|Title|Formula|Para|
                          ParaCont)*>
<!ELEMENT Title      - -  ((#PCDATA)|Empty|Link|Ref|Fig|FigCont|String|Title|StrCont|Formula|
                          Para|ParaCont)*>

<!ELEMENT FigCont    - -  (Empty|Link|Ref|Fig|FigCont|Title|String|StrCont|StrGrp|Formula|
                          Table)*>
<!ELEMENT Fig        - 0  EMPTY>
<!ELEMENT Ref        - -  ((#PCDATA)|Empty|Link|Ref|Fig|FigCont|String|StrCont|StrGrp|
                          Formula)*>
<!ATTLIST Ref        rid  IDREF  #IMPLIED>
<!ELEMENT Link       - 0  EMPTY>
<!ATTLIST Link       rid  IDREF  #REQUIRED>
<!ELEMENT Empty      - 0  EMPTY>

<!ENTITY % Table.def system 'table.def'>
<!ENTITY % Formula.def system 'formula.def'>
%Table.def;
%Formula.def;
```

The architectural form attributes can be specified in the document itself or in the DTD. If they are defined in the document, architectural form attributes for different base architectures are defined separately for every element instance, while in the latter case they are defined only once in the DTD in conjunction with the original element types. We have considered the latter case in our experiments

and examples in order to maintain a clear and easy-to-understand approach; see
Example 4 for an example of an architectural form attribute list.

Example 4. This example contains an architectural form attribute list, i.e., mapping, for a document [4] that uses the Book DTD of ISO 12083 and the base architecture DTD *VirtDoc* given in Example 3.[4]

```
<!ATTLIST book      VirtDoc    NAME #FIXED "VirtDoc">
<!ATTLIST front     VirtDoc    NAME #FIXED "SecGrp">
<!ATTLIST titlegrp  VirtDoc    NAME #FIXED "Title">
<!ATTLIST title     VirtDoc    NAME #FIXED "Title">
<!ATTLIST subtitle  VirtDoc    NAME #FIXED "String">
<!ATTLIST authgrp   VirtDoc    NAME #FIXED "StrGrp">
<!ATTLIST author    VirtDoc    NAME #FIXED "StrCont">
<!ATTLIST fname     VirtDoc    NAME #FIXED "String">
<!ATTLIST surname   VirtDoc    NAME #FIXED "String">
<!ATTLIST pubfront  VirtDoc    NAME #FIXED "ParaCont">
<!ATTLIST pubname   VirtDoc    NAME #FIXED "StrCont">
<!ATTLIST orgname   VirtDoc    NAME #FIXED "String">
<!ATTLIST city      VirtDoc    NAME #FIXED "String">
<!ATTLIST country   VirtDoc    NAME #FIXED "String">
<!ATTLIST cpyrt     VirtDoc    NAME #FIXED "StrGrp">
<!ATTLIST date      VirtDoc    NAME #FIXED "Title">
<!ATTLIST cpyrtnme  VirtDoc    NAME #FIXED "StrCont">
<!ATTLIST catalog   VirtDoc    NAME #FIXED "Para">
<!ATTLIST figgrp    VirtDoc    NAME #FIXED "FigCont">
<!ATTLIST fig       VirtDoc    NAME #FIXED "Fig">
<!ATTLIST ded       VirtDoc    NAME #FIXED "ParaCont">
<!ATTLIST p         VirtDoc    NAME #FIXED "Para">
<!ATTLIST preface   VirtDoc    NAME #FIXED "Section">
<!ATTLIST noteref   VirtDoc    NAME #FIXED "Ref">
<!ATTLIST body      VirtDoc    NAME #FIXED "SecGrp">
<!ATTLIST chapter   VirtDoc    NAME #FIXED "Section">
<!ATTLIST no        VirtDoc    NAME #FIXED "Title">
<!ATTLIST emph      VirtDoc    NAME #FIXED "String">
<!ATTLIST bq        VirtDoc    NAME #FIXED "ParaCont">
<!ATTLIST poem      VirtDoc    NAME #FIXED "StrGrp">
<!ATTLIST poemline  VirtDoc    NAME #FIXED "Title">
<!ATTLIST section   VirtDoc    NAME #FIXED "Section">
<!ATTLIST stanza    VirtDoc    NAME #FIXED "StrCont">
<!ATTLIST back      VirtDoc    NAME #FIXED "SecGrp">
<!ATTLIST notes     VirtDoc    NAME #FIXED "SecGrp">
<!ATTLIST note      VirtDoc    NAME #FIXED "ParaCont">
<!ATTLIST list      VirtDoc    NAME #FIXED "SecGrp">
<!ATTLIST head      VirtDoc    NAME #FIXED "Title">
<!ATTLIST item      VirtDoc    NAME #FIXED "ParaCont">

<!ENTITY % original.dtd PUBLIC "ISO 12083:1993//DTD Book//EN">
%original.dtd;
```

The classification was done using only one document [4]. An excerpt of the original document is presented in Appendix B. There are some minor differences between this mapping and the descriptions in Appendix A, which includes an idealistic mapping of the element types of the Book DTD of ISO 12083. This demonstrates that classification is dependent of the markup of the original document instances; typically DTDs are quite permissive, and allow the user some flexibility which may result in slightly different mappings for a given DTD between different document collections.

---

[4] Note that although we present only one mapping in our examples in this paper, it is possible to represent several mappings, based on different base architecture DTDs, in the same file.

5   Results of the Classification Experiments

We have implemented the classification method using Perl and TranSID, a transformation language developed in our group. In our experiments, we used eight document classes. The DTDs used include the Book DTD of ISO 12083[5], TEI DTD and TEI Lite DTD[6], and DocBook DTD[7]. The texts include poetry, novels and manuals. We also used a large collection of Finnish statutes and three Finnish textbooks on control engineering. The collection of the Finnish statutes has a size of hundreds of megabytes, whereas the rest of the collections is altogether approximately 40 megabytes of plain text.

Some unpredictable characteristics were found in the initial rounds of experiments. For instance, some title elements contained footnotes which in turn contained paragraphs. Thus, the base-DTD had to be modified after the first experiments; e.g., strings may contain paragraphs if the original DTD allows such a structure.

All the different document classes were classified, and the results are promising: it appears that the tree structure skeleton remains nicely after the classification process, and even almost all the titles were recognized; as an example, compare the documents in Appendices B (original document) and C (resulting architectural document). However, there are some areas that are to be developed, e.g., the recognition of tables and formulas, and the method for retaining original attributes in the architectural document and the meta-DTD.

6   Conclusions

We have addressed the problem of processing heterogenous SGML structures by introducing an element type classification method. The method analyzes document instances and document type definitions, and maps each SGML element type to one pre-defined generic class. The mapping of elements types into generic classes can be compared to the conversion of some structured form to the HTML format: the complexity of the structure is reduced. Opposite to HTML, the new document still has a non-trivial hierarchical structure. Moreover, the old element name can be stored to each element as an attribute, and hence, the original structure can be reconstructed.

We have implemented the method using Perl and our own transformation language TranSID. In our experiments, documents from several document types have been classified. In the near future we intend to evaluate the classification approach further in connection with our document assembly workbench SAW. The approach presented is simple and it can be further developed to gather more of the semantics of the source documents. However, a rather simple method may actually work, at least in unanticipated situations, more reliably.

---

[5] http://ftp.sunet.se/pub/text-processing/sgml/ISO12083/

[6] http://www.uic.edu/orgs/tei/

[7] http://www.ora.com/davenport/#docbook

Acknowledgments

This work has been supported by the Finnish Technology Development Centre (TEKES) and seven Finnish enterprises (Aamulehti Group, Edita, National Board of Education, WSOY, Helsinki Media, Lingsoft, and MTV3). Furthermore, this work has been partially supported by the Academy of Finland post-doctoral grant and the EC/TMR Marie Curie research training grant #ERBFMBICT972821 (Helena Ahonen), and grants by the 350th Anniversary Foundation of the University of Helsinki (Oskari Heinonen), the Finnish Cultural Foundation (Barbara Heikkinen) and the Nokia Foundation (Mika Klemettinen).

References

1. S. Abiteboul. Querying semi-structured data. In *Proceedings of the 6th International Conference on Database Theory, ICDT'97*, number 1186 in Lecture Notes in Computer Science, pages 1–18, Delphi, Greece, Jan. 1997. Springer-Verlag.
2. H. Ahonen, B. Heikkinen, O. Heinonen, J. Jaakkola, P. Kilpeläinen, and G. Lindén. Design and implementation of a document assembly workbench. In *Electronic Publishing, Artistic Imaging, and Digital Typography, Proceedings of the 7th International Conference on Electronic Publishing, EP'98*, number 1375 in Lecture Notes in Computer Science, Saint-Malo, France, Mar./Apr. 1998. Springer-Verlag.
3. H. Ahonen, B. Heikkinen, O. Heinonen, J. Jaakkola, P. Kilpeläinen, G. Lindén, and H. Mannila. Intelligent Assembly of Structured Documents. Technical Report C-1996-40, University of Helsinki, Department of Computer Science, Finland, June 1996.
4. R. Bordin. *Alice Freeman Palmer: The Evolution of a New Woman.* The University of Michigan Press, Ann Arbor, Michigan, USA, 1993. Available at http://www.press.umich.edu/bookhome/bordin/.
5. P. Buneman. Semistructured data: a tutorial. In *Proceedings of the 16th ACM SIGACT-SIGMOD-SIGART Symposium on Principles of Database Systems, PODS'97*, pages 117–121, Tucson, Arizona, USA, May 1997. ACM.
6. V. Christophides, M. Dörr, and I. Fundulaki. A semantic network approach to semi-structured documents repositories. In C. Peters and C. Thanos, editors, *Proceedings of the 1st European Conference on Research and Advanced Technology for Digital Libraries, ECDL'97*, number 1324 in Lecture Notes in Computer Science, pages 305–324, Pisa, Italy, Sept. 1997. Springer-Verlag.
7. ISO. *Information Processing — Text and Office Systems — Standard Generalized Markup Language (SGML), ISO 8879*, 1986.
8. ISO/IEC. *Hypermedia/Time-based Structuring Language (HyTime), 2nd Edition, ISO/IEC 10744*, 1997.
9. J. Jaakkola, P. Kilpeläinen, and G. Lindén. TranSID: An SGML tree transformation language. In J. Paakki, editor, *Proceedings of the Fifth Symposium on Programming Languages and Software Tools*, pages 72–83, Jyväskylä, Finland, June 1997. Technical Report C-1997-37, University of Helsinki, Department of Computer Science, Finland.
10. S. Nestorov, S. Abiteboul, and R. Motwani. Inferring structure in semistructured data. *SIGMOD Record*, 26(4):39–43, Dec. 1997.
11. D. Suciu. Management of semistructured data. *SIGMOD Record*, 26(4):4–7, Dec. 1997.

A   Element Class Descriptions

This table explains some of the characteristics of the generic element classes. The third column shows some element types of the Book DTD of ISO 12083 that typically map to the class of the first column. Square brackets ($[\cdot]$) in the second column indicate that the element class is allowed but implies bad markup style. len_{elem} is the average text length (in characters) of the element type's instances, and $len_{subtree}$ is the average text length of the subtrees of the element type's instances.

Class	Description	ISO 12083
Empty	Empty element.	toc
Link	Empty element which has an attribute of type IDREF.	noteref, fnoteref, figref, tableref, secref, appref, citeref, glosref, indexref
Ref	$0 < len_{elem} \leq 60$; element has an attribute of type IDREF.	
Fig	Empty element which has an attribute of type graphics NOTATION.	fig
FigCont	$len_{elem} = 0$; children may be of class Empty/Link/Ref/Fig/FigCont/ Formula / dFormula / Table / String / Title/StrCont/StrGrp; at least one child is Fig; typically contains Figs and Strings.	figgrp
Formula	Inline formula; Fig defined as Formula or marked up with some standard like HTML Math.	formula
dFormula	Display formula; Fig defined as dFormula or marked up with some standard like HTML Math.	dformula
Table	Table of some standard like CALS or HTML.	table
String	$0 < len_{elem} \leq 60$; children may be of class Empty/Link/Ref/Fig/ [FigCont] / Formula / String / [Title / Para/ParaCont].	emph, superscr, subscr, fname, surname, date, orgname, city, country, sertitle, subtitle, othinfo, poemline
Title	Originally classified as String or StrCont; Title is the first child in upper level elements like Section or ParaCont.	title, titlegrp, head, no

Class	Description	ISO 12083
StrCont	$len_{elem} = 0$; children may be of class Empty / Link / Ref / [Fig] / FigCont / Formula / String / Title / [StrCont]; at least one child is String; typically contains Strings.	author, pubname, corpauth, cpyrtnme, poem
StrGrp	$len_{elem} = 0$; children may be of class Empty / Link / Ref / [Fig] / FigCont / Formula / dFormula / Table / String / Title / StrCont / StrGrp; subtrees of children contain Strings; typically contains StrConts and StrGrps.	authgrp, cpyrt, citation, biblist
Para	$60 < len_{elem} \leq 1000$; children may not be of class Section/SecGrp/VirtDoc.	p
ParaCont	$len_{elem} = 0$; children may not be of class Section/SecGrp/VirtDoc; at least one child is Para; typically contains Paras.	item, dd, footnote, note, bq, pubfront
ParaGrp	$len_{elem} = 0$; children may not be of class Para/Section/SecGrp/ VirtDoc; subtrees of children contain Paras; typically contains ParaConts and ParaGrps.	list, deflist
Section	$len_{subtree} > 1000$; children may be of any class other than VirtDoc; at least one child is Para; typically contains Paras and lower level Sections; attribute *level* (l) indicates the level in Section hierachy.	chapter ($l = 1$), section ($l = 2$), subsect1 ($l = 3$), subsect2 ($l = 4$), appendix ($l = 1$), afterwrd ($l = 1$), foreword ($l = 1$), preface ($l = 1$)
SecGrp	$len_{subtree} > 1000$; $len_{elem} = 0$; children may be of any class other than Para; typically contains Sections.	front, body, part, appmat, back
VirtDoc	The root of the document; children may be of any class other than VirtDoc.	book

B Original Document

```
<BOOK>
  <FRONT>
    <TITLEGRP><TITLE>Alice Freeman Palmer</TITLE>
      <SUBTITLE>The Evolution of a New Woman</SUBTITLE></TITLEGRP>
    <AUTHGRP><AUTHOR><FNAME>Ruth </FNAME>
      <SURNAME>Bordin</SURNAME></AUTHOR></AUTHGRP>
    ...
    <PREFACE><TITLE>Preface</TITLE>
      <P>The research for this biography of Alice Freeman Palmer began...</P>
      <P>Alice Freeman Palmer's career was distinguished and...</P>
      ...
      <P>... partner in resolving my own dilemma.</P></PREFACE>
  </FRONT>
  <BODY>
    <CHAPTER ID="CH01"><NO>1</NO><TITLE>The New Woman</TITLE>
      <P>At the turn of the century, Alice Freeman Palmer, ...</P>
      <P>Her role in higher education expanded, rather than...</P>
      ...
      <P>The phrase <EMPH TYPE="2">New Woman</EMPH> was coined originally...</P>
      ...
    </CHAPTER>
    <CHAPTER ID="CH02"><NO>2</NO><TITLE>Genesis</TITLE>...</CHAPTER>
    <CHAPTER ID="CH03"><NO>3</NO><TITLE>Commitment</TITLE>...</CHAPTER>
    <CHAPTER ID="CH04"><NO>4</NO><TITLE>Crucible</TITLE>
      <P>When Alice Freeman graduated from the University of Michigan...</P>
      ...
      <SECTION><NO>1</NO>
        <P>Alice began the crucible years happily enough. She...</P>
        ...
        <P>Alice Freeman needed cash desperately. She was in debt. ...
          She described her experience at Lake Geneva in a letter to her friend
          Lucy Andrews.
          <BQ><P>The days have been very trying to me for...</P></BQ>
          She went on to describe her work:
          <BQ><P>. . . it isn't so very hard or wearing. ...</P></BQ>
          ...
        </P>
        ...
        <P>... republican institutions in the eyes of Europe.</P>
      </SECTION>
      <SECTION><NO>2</NO>
        <P>In June Alice Freeman was finally free of Lake Geneva Seminary. ...</P>
        ...
      </SECTION>
    </CHAPTER>
    <CHAPTER ID="CH05"><NO>5</NO><TITLE>Vocation</TITLE>
      <P>In June of 1879, Alice Freeman accepted the professorship of history
        at Wellesley College. ...</P>
      <SECTION><NO>1</NO>
        <P>We do not know precisely why Henry Durant first attempted...</P>
        ...
      </SECTION>
      <SECTION><NO>2</NO>...</SECTION>
      ...
      <SECTION><NO>5</NO>...</SECTION>
    </CHAPTER>
    <CHAPTER ID="CH06"><NO>6</NO><TITLE>Fulfillment</TITLE>...</CHAPTER>
    ...
    <CHAPTER ID="CH10"><NO>10</NO><TITLE>Resolution</TITLE>...</CHAPTER>
  </BODY>
  <BACK>
    ...
    <NOTES><TITLE>Bibliography</TITLE>
      ...
      <LIST><HEAD>Published Materials</HEAD>
        ...
        <ITEM><P>Donnan, Elizabeth. "Henry Fowle Durant."
          <EMPH TYPE="2">Dictionary of American Biography</EMPH>.
          3:541&ndash;42.</P></ITEM>
        ...
      </LIST>
      ...
    </NOTES>
  </BACK>
</BOOK>
```

C   Architectural Document

```
<VIRTDOC>
  <SECGRP>
    <TITLE><TITLE>Alice Freeman Palmer</TITLE>
      <STRING>The Evolution of a New Woman</STRING></TITLE>
    <STRGRP><STRCONT><STRING>Ruth </STRING>
      <STRING>Bordin</STRING></STRCONT></STRGRP>
    ...
    <SECTION><TITLE>Preface</TITLE>
      <PARA>The research for this biography of Alice Freeman Palmer began...</PARA>
      <PARA>Alice Freeman Palmer's career was distinguished and certainly...</PARA>
      ...
      <PARA>... partner in resolving my own dilemma.</PARA></SECTION>
  </SECGRP>
  <SECGRP>
    <SECTION><TITLE>1</TITLE><TITLE>The New Woman</TITLE>
      <PARA>At the turn of the century, Alice Freeman Palmer, ...</PARA>
      <PARA>Her role in higher education expanded, rather than...</PARA>
      ...
      <PARA>The phrase <STRING>New Woman</STRING> was coined originally...</PARA>
      ...
    </SECTION>
    <SECTION><TITLE>2</TITLE><TITLE>Genesis</TITLE>...</SECTION>
    <SECTION><TITLE>3</TITLE><TITLE>Commitment</TITLE>...</SECTION>
    <SECTION><TITLE>4</TITLE><TITLE>Crucible</TITLE>
      <PARA>When Alice Freeman graduated from the University of Michigan...</PARA>
      ...
      <SECTION><TITLE>1</TITLE>
        <PARA>Alice began the crucible years happily enough. She...</PARA>
        ...
        <PARA>Alice Freeman needed cash desperately. She was in debt. ...
          She described her experience at Lake Geneva in a letter to her friend
          Lucy Andrews.
          <PARACONT><PARA>The days have been very trying to me for...</PARA></PARACONT>
          She went on to describe her work:
          <PARACONT><PARA>. . . it isn't so very hard or wearing. ...</PARA></PARACONT>
          ...
        </PARA>
        ...
        <PARA>... republican institutions in the eyes of Europe.</PARA>
      </SECTION>
      <SECTION><TITLE>2</TITLE>
        <PARA>In June Alice Freeman was finally free of Lake Geneva Seminary. ...</PARA>
        ...
      </SECTION>
    </SECTION>
    <SECTION><TITLE>5</TITLE><TITLE>Vocation</TITLE>
      <PARA>In June of 1879, Alice Freeman accepted the professorship of history
        at Wellesley College. ...</PARA>
      <SECTION><TITLE>1</TITLE>
        <PARA>We do not know precisely why Henry Durant first attempted...</PARA>
        ...
      </SECTION>
      <SECTION><TITLE>2</TITLE>...</SECTION>
      ...
      <SECTION><TITLE>5</TITLE>...</SECTION>
    </SECTION>
    <SECTION><TITLE>6</TITLE><TITLE>Fulfillment</TITLE>...</SECTION>
    ...
    <SECTION><TITLE>10</TITLE><TITLE>Resolution</TITLE>...</SECTION>
  </SECGRP>
  <SECGRP>
    ...
    <SECGRP><TITLE>Bibliography</TITLE>
      ...
      <SECGRP><TITLE>Published Materials</TITLE>
        ...
        <PARACONT><PARA>Donnan, Elizabeth. "Henry Fowle Durant."
          <STRING>Dictionary of American Biography</STRING>.
          3:541&ndash;42.</PARA></PARACONT>
        ...
      </SECGRP>
      ...
    </SECGRP>
    ...
  </SECGRP>
</VIRTDOC>
```

Using Document Relationships for Better Answers

Mingfang Wu[1] and Ross Wilkinson[2]

[1] Department of Computer Science, Royal Melbourne Institute of Technology, 723
Swanston St., Carlton 3053, Melbourne, Australia
`ming@cs.rmit.edu.au`
[2] Mathematical and Information Sciences, CSIRO and Research Data Network
Cooperative Research Centre, 723 Swanston St., Carlton 3053 Melbourne, Australia
`Ross.Wilkinson@cmis.csiro.au`

Abstract. In most retrieval systems the answer to a query is a ranked list of documents. There is little information about the ranking and no support for exploring the relationships that may exist between the documents. In this paper we consider the use of clustering answers to better support users satisfying their information needs. We show how clustering reflects the nature of some information needs, and how the clustering can be used to find more relevant documents than would be the case using simple lists. This work contributes to our approach of building answers to information needs, rather than simply providing lists.

1 Introduction

The question answering process includes three stages: question formulation, information gathering, and answer analysis/synthesis [24]. In the question formulation stage, a user transfers an actual, but unexpressed need for information into a query as presented to a information system [19]. In the information gathering stage, a user may try to gather all potentially relevant documents. In the answer analysis/synthesis stage, the user will examine and analyze those collected documents to find out any piece of relevant information which could be used to answer the question, then synthesize this information for different purposes.

Question formulation is carried out when a person describes their information need in the query languages of Information Retrieval (IR) systems. These systems can serve well for the stage two of question answering process, i.e. the collection of potentially relevant documents. However, a list of ranked documents delivered from this stage can seldom be used as an answer to a user's question. The top ranked documents may not necessarily be relevant to a user's question, because the rank of a retrieved document in the list is usually determined by the relative frequency of query words appearing in a document. It will take a user much more effort to navigate, orient, search and extract useful information.

In this paper we concentrate on supporting the third stage of question answering by clustering the highly ranked documents that have been identified by the IR system. Clustering serves two purposes: it shows the user information about the relationships between documents, and also it can be used as a navigational aid in exploring the answer space. We demonstrate the utility of this approach by showing that viewing the documents by taking into account both clustering information and rank information leads to improved retrieval performance. We believe that the user is better able to understand the answer space as well, however we have not conducted experiments to test this.

In our experiment we simulate the path a user might take through the answer space by re-ordering the documents. Suppose a user has to find out which factors led to a major event occurring. In this task we have to find each of these factors, but not fully analyze every aspect. Thus we try to consider how a user might visit documents if clustering information is available. The re-ordering approach is based on the hypothesis that:

– the retrieved documents have some coherent relationships among them, which can be used to classify them into several groups [9], where each group of documents has a similar aspect of the information need, and subsequently, this group of documents could be represented by or substituted by a typical document from the group, or some summary of this group.

An experiment has been designed and implemented to examine the hypothesis and to test the re-ordering methods. As in the TREC interactive task [8], aspectual recall is used as the criteria for measuring and comparing this re-ordered list against the original ranked list produced by a information retrieval system, MG [23]. Aspectual retrieval simply counts how many aspects are discovered after viewing n documents. The experimental results show that the list obtained using interactive ranking method is better than the list obtained using an automatic cluster ranking method and the original ranked list.

The rest of this paper is organized as follows. Section 2 gives a description of answer organization and presentation. Section 3 introduces various reordering algorithms. Section 4 describes an experiment conducted to evaluate reordered lists from various reordering algorithms, and section 5 gives the conclusion.

2   Answer Organization and Presentation

In the process of constructing an answer by searching information from a set of documents, a user may use various tactics such as: browsing, starting, differentiating (filtering or discriminating), assimilating, and extracting [2]. The user may browse the documents purposefully by starting with an concrete example of a concept, keyword, or a document that symbolizes the character of the information need, filter those documents that have a higher likelihood of containing relevant information from those have a lower likelihood, read those documents in detail to identify specific information, and finally, gather the identified information for action (for example, writing a report, or inferring some facts).

Accordingly, our approach towards the organization of retrieved documents involves two major activities: *grouping* and *ordering* [7]. Grouping refers to the assignment of individual retrieved documents to clusters on the base of shared relationships, that is, to help a user browse and differentiate document sets. Ordering refers to the ranking of documents within and among clusters. Grouping and ordering together may give a user a good starting point that leads to the areas of interest.

There are various shared relationships among documents which could be used to group them, for example: we can group documents according to authors, date, or keywords. In this paper, we will concentrate on grouping documents into content oriented clusters in order to address the user's information need for finding various aspects of a question. For this purpose, clustering methods can be used.

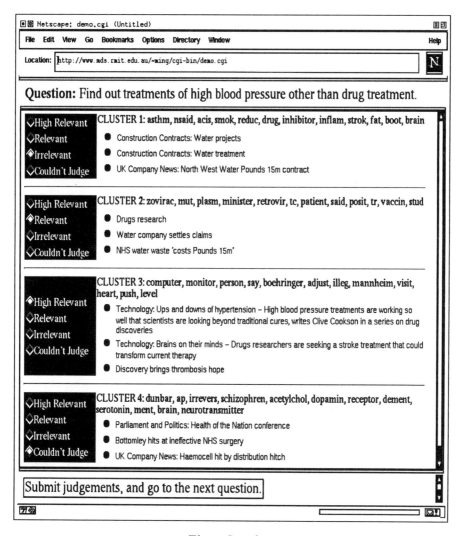

Fig. 1. Interface

The objective of cluster analysis is to find a convenient and valid organization of the data [12]. It was used in IR to cluster all documents in a database into content oriented clusters, thus enhance search and retrieval performance by matching the query to the cluster centroid [22]. Recently, it has also been used to dynamically group retrieved documents after each search, aiming to improve the presentation of retrieval results and to facilitate user's browsing [5, 11, 10, 14]. Here, the research concentrated on investigating if documents which are deemed to be about related topics are grouped together, thus differentiating those relevant documents from non-relevant documents. However, from the question answering viewpoint, we will need to go further to cluster relevant documents around an aspect. If documents could be grouped about the same aspect, then those documents in the same cluster should be inter-substitutable in terms of the aspect. This information will be very useful in filtering out those documents with various aspects from retrieved results.

We can then adopt various strategies to present clustered results for different purposes, as a user's information need which may vary from fact finding to browsing [1, 13, 21]. For example, in the Scatter/Gather approach [10], all clusters of documents, together with keywords that describe a cluster, are presented to a user for browsing; alternatively, a list of extracted aspects could satisfy user's need for fact finding. A combined approach might be to allow a user to locate a specific fact while enabling him or her to get the context of this fact. Until we are able to effectively synthesize answers, we will always be viewing documents – clustering information simply guides our path through the documents.

The aim of reordering could be to present a user with a screen sized, synthesized list of documents which could represent each aspect of a question, while each document may maintain links to other documents on a similar aspect or in the same cluster. This screen of information is a first step to a concise summary of retrieved information. With it, a user could locate a specific fact, or take it as a starting point to browse the clustered retrieved documents. The next section will discuss how to construct such a list by using clustering information.

3   Reordering Algorithm

When we construct a screen of document representatives by using clustering information, we need to determine which retrieved documents are to be included and in what order. An easy way could be to pick one document from each cluster – if the clustering algorithm is perfect and clusters exactly on aspects. However not all retrieved documents are relevant to the question, and clustering is not perfect. Those documents with relevant aspects may be distributed unevenly among clusters. Therefore each cluster, and documents in a cluster, may not have equal importance to the user's information need. We need to rank clusters and documents in a cluster, then decide which documents will be selected according to a weighting scheme. In this section, we will present the schemes to form clusters, to rank clusters, and strategies to select documents from each cluster.

3.1 Initial Ranking Algorithm

We initially rank the documents using a often used version of the cosine measure:

$$cos(q, d) = \frac{\sum_{t \in q \wedge d}(w_{q,t} \cdot w_{d,t})}{\sqrt{\left(\sum_{t \in q}(w_{q,t})^2 \cdot \sum_{t \in d}(w_{d,t})^2\right)}}$$

with weights that have been shown to be robust and give good retrieval performance [3]: $w_{q,t} = log(N/f_t) + 1$ and $w_{d,t} = log(f_{d,t} + 1)$ where $f_{x,t}$ is the frequency of t in x, where x is either q or d, N is the number of documents in the collection, and f_t is the number of documents containing t.

The top M ranked documents are then selected for clustering.

3.2 Clustering Algorithm

There are a wide variety of document clustering algorithms available [6, 20, 16]; they can be broadly classified into two categories: the hierarchical and the non-hierarchical clustering methods. Our purpose of using a cluster method is to group and order a set of documents with regard to certain aspects. The concept of documents being "about" a certain aspect is already inexact, so hierarchically structuring is probably not appropriate in this case [14]. We thus adopted a non-hierarchical single-pass algorithm. Though the efficiency of clustering is important [5, 18], we are only clustering a small number of documents, so we concentrated more on the effectiveness of clustering in this paper. A single-pass algorithm was implemented and used. To avoid document order dependence, a second pass was also conducted.

3.3 The Ranking of Clusters

Two approaches are examined: the automatic cluster ranking approach and the interactive cluster ranking approach.

In the automatic cluster ranking approach, clusters are ranked automatically according to the similarity of each cluster's centroid to the query. This kind of ranking approach has also been used in many situations [4, 15, 17]. However, the automatic cluster ranking approach may not reflect a user's real information needs, because it is simply based on the similarity of a cluster's centroid to a query.

In the interactive cluster ranking approach, clusters are ranked manually according to the user's judgement. An experiment on the interactive cluster ranking method has been developed and conducted. Figure. 1 shows a snapshot of the experiment. This interactive cluster ranking method will be used to evaluate the effectiveness of automatic cluster ranking approach.

Within a cluster, a document can be ranked according to its nearness to the query or to cluster's centroid. Our experiment showed that the ranking results based on the document nearness to the query is better than nearness to the cluster's centroid. Other experiments have also found this to be the case [10]. We adopted document nearness to the query as the criteria to order documents within a cluster.

3.4 Document Selection

After clustering, documents are organized into a list of clusters. Therefore, any document will have two ranks: the rank of its cluster, and its rank in the cluster. These two ranks will be used to determine the selection of documents and the rank of documents in the synthesized list. This attempts to reflect a user's path through the retrieved documents. That is, we will need to construct a one dimensional list from a two dimensional matrix of ranks.

There is no universal approach to convert this two dimensional matrix into a linear list. We need to develop a weighting scheme to differentiate the importance of the rank among clusters and within clusters. The following three schemes were used and tested to rank documents in a list to be constructed.

- **Depth-first** weighting: In this weighting, the rank of a cluster has primary preference, and then the rank of a document within a cluster has secondary preference. This means all documents will be taken from one cluster before another cluster. This will favour all those documents in highly ranked clusters.
- **Width-first** weighting (round robin): Opposite to the depth-first one, in this weight, the rank of a document within a cluster has primary preference, while the rank of a cluster has secondary preference. In this scheme, documents will be taken from each cluster in turn. This will favour highly ranked documents in all clusters.
- **Weighted round robin** weighting: The weight is determined by combining the ranks. It is a balance between the above two weighting schemes: one prefers the rank of a document, one the rank of a cluster. Here, highly ranked documents in highly ranked clusters get more chance to score best, but highly ranked documents in lowly ranked cluster are mixed with low ranked documents in highly ranked clusters.

4 Experiment

In this experiment we aim to carry out a task of finding all aspects of an information need, rather than simply finding relevant documents. Thus we must construct a list of document representatives to cover more aspects at the top of a list compared to the original ranked list. In this section, we evaluate the reordered list resulting from various reordering algorithms discussed in section 3.

4.1 Experiment Setup

Twelve interactive TREC topics from TREC5 [8] are used since they cover the available aspect judgements. The corresponding queries are used first to retrieve the top 30 documents according to the cosine measure as implemented in MG, then the top 50 words are extracted as an expanded query to retrieve the top 300 documents. These 300 documents are then used as the basis for clustering.

In the interactive cluster ranking approach, four postgraduate students volunteered to take part in the experiment. Each of them judged the relevance of clusters for 6 topics, with each topic judged by two users to reduce user differences. The final cluster ranking for each topic is based on the average judgement of two users.

4.2 Evaluation and Discussion

In IR, recall and precision are generally used to evaluate a system's performance. In this experiment, we go further: we not only find relevant documents, also why the documents are relevant. Therefore, we need to determine the aspectual recall, that is the proportion of aspects retrieved for each query. The average aspectual recall of twelve topics is used to evaluate and compare three document selections with both clustering ranking methods, and the original ranked list with two lists resulting from best document selection in each cluster ranking method.

Table 1. Comparison of average aspectual recall for three document selection schemes in automatic cluster ranking method.

Docs.	Average Aspectual Recall		
	Depth-first	Width-first	Weighted round robin
5	0.085	0.103	0.102
10	0.129	0.143	0.167
15	0.162	0.210	0.188
20	0.191	0.244	0.276

Table 2. Comparison of average aspectual recall for three document selection schemes in interactive cluster ranking method.

Docs.	Average Aspectual Recall		
	Depth-first	Width-first	Weighted round robin
5	0.144	0.148	0.159
10	0.197	0.218	0.231
15	0.262	0.250	0.267
20	0.296	0.273	0.295

Table 3. Overall comparison of aspectual recall for weighted round robin with simple ranking.

	Average Aspectual Recall		
Docs.	Auto-ranked	Inter-ranked	Sim-ranked
5	0.102	0.159	0.133
10	0.167	0.231	0.176
15	0.188	0.267	0.226
20	0.276	0.295	0.248

As we want to present a user a screen of representative documents covering the aspects of the topic, selecting 15 documents might be adequate. For all lists, the average aspectual recall at 5, 10, 15, and 20 documents retrieved are calculated and compared.

Tables 1 and 2 show the comparison from three document selection schemes corresponding to automatic cluster ranking method and interactive cluster ranking method respectively. In both cases, average aspectual recall for depth-first selection is lower than that for width-first, and weighted round robin selection. That might be because by this method, documents in low ranked clusters might not get chance to be selected. For example, if first cluster contains 20 documents, then none of the documents in the rest clusters can be selected. Intuitively, documents from the same cluster should contain less aspects than documents from different clusters. Getting documents from more clusters might be good for extracting various aspects, but it should avoid to get documents from those clusters that might not contain any relevant document or aspect.

The lists obtained by using weighted round robin selection with different cluster ranking methods are chosen to compare with the original ranked list, as shown in Table 3. The automatic cluster rank approach is much poorer than the interactive cluster rank approach – even lower than the original ranked list, though four subjects were not satisfied with the description of clusters (10 word stems and titles of three documents). We thus see that even very simple interfaces that allow users to select clusters has a very beneficial effect – users are able to select clusters that have relevant documents, and importantly determine that clusters that do not have relevant documents.

5   Conclusions and Further Work

In this paper, we have investigated richer ways of answering queries. We have done this by clustering highly ranked documents and thus provided users with a way of navigating the answer space. We have seen that users can successfully identify the nature of these clusters by using this clustering information to improve aspectual recall. Three weighting schemes were used to rank documents. The lists from three weighting schemes were compared after examining different numbers of documents. A weighting scheme taking into account both document ranking and cluster ranking is used to comparing two cluster ranking methods with original ranked list. The result shows that the average aspectual recall is higher for the interactive cluster ranking approach. This might suggest that it is hard to find automatic reordering method without user's feedback. It also shows that users are able to use clusters effectively in navigating the answer space.

The results also point to ways to improve our work in extracting various aspects from retrieved documents and a way to improve the presentation. In future, we will investigate how to improve the clustering strategy. One approach might break documents into small chunks, then cluster these small chunks. This will also address the issue of presenting information or facts instead of documents. Importantly, we will further investigate methods of presenting retrieved documents to better satisfy user's information needs. Finally we will investigate methods of synthesizing answers using ranking, clustering, and summarization, so that IR systems can more truly satisfy information needs, rather than identify potentially relevant documents.

Acknowledgements

The work reported in this paper has been partially funded by the Cooperative Research Centers Program through the Department of the Prime Minister and Cabinet of Australia, and by the Australian Research Council.

References

1. N. J. Belkin, P. G. Marchetti, and C. CooL. Braque: Design of an interface to support user interaction in inform ation retrieval. Information Processing and Management, 29(3):325–344, 1993.
2. M.E. Brown. A general model of information-seeking behavior. Journal of the American Society for Information Science, 42(1):9–14, 1991.
3. C. Buckley, G. Salton, and J. Allan. The effect of adding relevance information in a relevance feedback environment. In Proceedings of the 17th Annual International ACM SIGIR Conference on Research and Development in Information Retrieval, pages 292–300, 1994.
4. W. B. Croft. A model of cluster searching based on classification. Information Systems, 5:189–195, 1980.
5. J.O. Cutting, D.R. Pedersen, D. Karger, and J.W. Tukey. Scatter/gather: A cluster-based approach to browsing large document collections. In Proceedings of the 15th Annual International ACM SIGIR Conference on Research and Development in Information Retrieval, pages 318–329, 1992.
6. W.B. Frakes and . Baeza-Yates. Information Retrieval: Data Structures and Algorithms. Prentice-Hall, 1992.
7. J.I.B. Gonzales. A theory of organization. In The 12th Annual International Conference on Systems Documentation, pages 145–155, Alberta, Canada, 1994. ACM.
8. D. Harman and E. Vorhees, editors. Proceedings of the Fifth Text Retrieval Conference, number 500–238 in NIST Special Publication, Gaithersburg, Maryland, 1996. Department of Commerce, National Institute of Standards and Technology.

9. R.M. Hayes. Mathematical Models in Information Retrieval. McGraw-Hill, New York, 1963.
10. M.A. Hearst and J.O. Pedersen. Re-examining the cluster hypothesis: Scatter/gather on retrieval results. In Proceedings of the 19th Annual International ACM SIGIR Conference on Research and Development in Information Retrieval, 1996.
11. M.A. Hearst, J.O. Pedersen, P. Pirolli, and H. Schutze. Xerox site report: Four TREC-4 tracks. In D. Harman, editor, Proceedings of the Fourth Text Retrieval Conference, 1995.
12. A.K. Jain and R.C. Dubes. Algorithms for Clustering Data. Prentice Hall, 1988.
13. G. Marchionini and B. Shneiderman. Finding facts vs. browsing knowledge in hypertext systems. IEEE Computer, 21(1):70–80, 1988.
14. Daniel E. Rose, Richard Mander, Tim Oren, Dulce B. Poncelon, Gitta Salo man, and Yin Yin Wong. Content awareness in a file system interface: Implementing the "pile" metaphor for organizing information. In Proceedings of the 16th Annual International ACM SIGIR Conference on Research and Development in Information Retrieval, pages 260–269, 1993.
15. G. Salton. Cluster search strategies and the optimization of retrieval effectiveness. In G. Salton, editor, The SMART Retrieval System, pages 223–242. Prentice Hall, 1971.
16. G. Salton. Automatic Text Processing. Addison-Wesley, Reading, Massachusetts, 1989.
17. H. Schutze and C. Silverstein. Projections for efficient document clustering. In Proceedings of the 20th Annual International ACM SIGIR Conference on Research and Development in Information Retrieval, pages 74–81, 1997.
18. C. Silverstein and J.O. Pedersen. Almost-constant-time clustering of arbitrary corpus subsets. In Proceedings of the 20th Annual International ACM SIGIR Conference on Research and Development in Information Retrieval, pages 60–66, 1997.
19. R.S. Taylor. The process of asking questions. American Documentation, pages 391–396, October 1962.
20. C. J. van Rijsbergen. Information Retrieval. Butterworths, London, 1979.
21. R. Wilkinson and M. Fuller. Integrated information access via structure. In M. Agosti and A. Smeaton, editors, Hypertext and Information Retrieval, pages 257–271. Kluwer, Boston, U.S.A., 1996.
22. P. Willett. Recent trends in hierarchic document clustering: A critical review. Information Processing and Management, 24(5):577–591, 1988.
23. I.H. Witten, A. Moffat, and T.C. Bell. Managing Gigabytes: Compressing and Indexing Documents and Images. Van Nostrand Reinhold, New York, 1994.
24. M. Wu and M.S. Fuller. Supporting the answering process. In J. Thom, editor, Proceeding of the Second Australian Document Computing Symposium, pages 65–73, Melbourne, Australia, 1997.

Generating, Visualizing, and Evaluating High-Quality Clusters for Information Organization

Javed Aslam, Katya Pelekhov, and Daniela Rus

Department of Computer Science, Dartmouth College, Hanover NH 03755
{jaa,katya,rus}@cs.dartmouth.edu

Abstract. We present and analyze the star clustering algorithm. We discuss an implementation of this algorithm that supports browsing and document retrieval through information organization. We define three parameters for evaluating a clustering algorithm to measure the topic separation and topic aggregation achieved by the algorithm. In the absence of benchmarks, we present a method for randomly generating clustering data. Data from our user study shows evidence that the star algorithm is effective for organizing information.

1 Introduction

Modern information systems have vast amounts of unorganized data. Users often don't know what they need until they need it. In dynamic, time-pressured situations such as emergency relief for weather disasters, presenting the results of a query as a ranked list of hundreds of titles is ineffective. To cull the critical information out of a large set of potentially useful sources we need methods for organizing as accurately as possible the data and ways of visualizing this organization flexibly.

We present a paradigm for organizing data that can be used as a pre-processing step in a static information system or as a post-processing step on the specific documents retrieved by a query. As a pre-processor, this system assists users with deciding how to browse the corpus by highlighting relevant topics and irrelevant subtopics. Such clustered data is useful for narrowing down the corpus over which detailed queries can be formulated. As a post-processor, this system classifies the retrieved data into clusters that capture topic categories and subcategories.

Our clustering method is called the star algorithm. The star algorithm gives a hierarchical organization of a collection into clusters. Each level in the hierarchy is determined by a threshold for the minimum similarity between pairs of documents within a cluster at that particular level in the hierarchy. This method conveys the topic-subtopic structure of the corpus according to the similarity measure used. Our implementation uses a modification of the Smart [Sal91] system and the underlying cosine metric. The star algorithm is accurate in that it produces dense clusters that approximate cliques with provable guarantees on the pairwise similarity between cluster documents, yet are computable in $O(N^2)$, where N is the number of documents. The documents in each cluster are tightly inter-related and a minimum similarity distance between all the document pairs in the cluster is guaranteed. This resulting structure reflects the underlying topic structure of the data. A topic summary for each cluster is provided by the center of the underlying star for the cluster.

To examine the performance of the star information organization system we developed a visualization method for data organized in clusters that presents users with three views of the data: a list of text titles; a Euclidean projection of the clusters in the plane as disks (of radius proportional to the size of the cluster) that are separated by distances proportional to the similarity distance between the clusters, and a graph that shows the similarity relationships between the documents. The user can examine each view and select individual objects in the view. For instance, the user may select the largest disk in the projection window. This causes the titles of the documents and their corresponding vertices to be highlighted in the title and graph views. The user may adjust interactively the thresholding parameter for clustering.

To evaluate the performance of this organization system we have defined a precision-recall measure for clustering. We also identified that the intersection point between the *precision curve* and the *recall curve* is the *critical point* for measuring the overall performance for information organization tasks. In the absence of benchmarks for clustering we developed two methods for randomly generating benchmarks. We measured the precision-recall of our algorithm against this data and found evidence that our algorithm has a high expected critical point. Depending on how much noise there is in the data, this value is at least 0.8. To validate these results, we did a user study on a collection of technical reports. We compared the user clusters against the system clusters and found further evidence that the star algorithm has good performance.

The experimental data we gathered and our user studies give strong positive evidence that clustering is a useful method for applications that require organizing data according to topic. Such applications typically require the algorithm to have high recall, as in the case of browsing and data reduction. Hearst and Pedersen [HP96] have already provided evidence that the clustering mechanism of Scatter/Gather is useful for high-recall tasks. Scatter/Gather uses fractionation to compute nearest-neighbour clusters. It is expected to produce clusters with loosely connected documents. Our clustering method trades-off performance for accuracy and yields tightly connected clusters. This, along with our preliminary experimental studies, encourages us to think that clustering algorithms with guarantees on the accuracy of the clusters will support the cluster hypothesis and thus assist in tasks that require high precision.

This paper is organized as follows. We first review related work. We then introduce our clustering algorithms. We continue by describing our implementation and visualization. Finally, we explain our performance measures and discuss experimental data.

2   Previous Work

There has been extensive research on clustering and applications to many do-
mains. For a good overview see [JD88]. For a good overview of using clustering
in information retrieval see [Wil88].

The use of clustering in information retrieval was mostly driven by the cluster
hypothesis [Rij79] which states that relevant documents tend to be more closely
related to each other than to non-relevant documents. Efforts have been made to
find whether the cluster hypothesis is valid. Voorhees [Voo85] discusses a way of
evaluating whether the cluster hypothesis holds and shows negative results. Croft
[Cro80] describes a method for bottom-up cluster search that could be shown
to outperform a full ranking system for the Cranfield collection. Willett's study
[Wil88] shows that the methods he surveys do not outperform non-clustered
search methods. In [JR71] Jardine and van Rijsbergen show some evidence that
search results could be improved by clustering. Hearst and Pedersen [HP96] re-
examine the cluster hypothesis and conclude that it holds for tasks that require
high recall, such as browsing.

Our work on clustering presented in this paper provides further evidence
that clustering is good for applications where the recall is important. We also
show that by trading off some of the performance of a fast system such as Scat-
ter/Gather[1] [CKP93] with computation to ensure cluster accuracy, (that is, to
guarantee a minimum similarity between all pairs of documents in a cluster)
clusters can also be good for tasks where precision is important. To compute accurate clusters, we formalize clustering as covering graphs by cliques. Covering
by cliques is NP-complete, and thus intractable for large document collections.
Recent graph-theoretic results have shown that the problem can't even be ap-
proximated in polynomial time [LY94,Zuc93]. Recent results for covering graphs
by dense subgraphs [KP93] are encouraging. We used a cover by dense subgraphs
that are star-shaped[2]. We show that this algorithm is an accurate and efficient
approximation of cliques, propose a measure for the quality of the clusters, and
provide experimental data.

3   Clustering Applications

The main application we have in mind for clustering is in information organization. Information organization can be used for browsing. If the clusters capture
the topic structure of the collection, organization can also be used to narrow the
search domain of a query and to organize the results retrieved in response to a
query. We also believe that tightly connected clusters (unlike loosely connected
clusters such as those obtained by a nearest-neighbour method or a single link
method) can also be used to improve retrieval as the cluster hypothesis suggests,
by returning the clusters corresponding to the top-most ranked documents. For

---

[1] Scatter/Gather uses fractionation to compute nearest-neighbor clusters.

[2] In [SJJ70] stars were also identified to be potentially useful for clustering.

our star-algorithm, an alternative is to return an entire cluster only when a top-ranked document is the center of a star. We are currently collecting data for this application.

4   Our Clustering Method

In this section we motivate and present two algorithms for organizing information systems. The first of our algorithms is very simple and efficient, and our second algorithm, while somewhat slower, has the advantage of being more accurate.

We formulate our problem by representing an information system by its *similarity graph*. A similarity graph is an undirected, weighted graph $G = (V, E, w)$ where vertices in the graph correspond to documents and each weighted edge in the graph corresponds to a measure of similarity between two documents. We measure the similarity between two documents by using the cosine metric in the vector space model of the Smart information retrieval system [Sal91,SM83]. G is a complete graph with edges of varying weight. An organization of the graph that produces reliable clusters of similarity σ (*i.e.*, clusters where documents pairwise have similarities of at least σ) can be obtained by performing a *minimum clique cover* of all edges whose weights are above the threshold σ. The following algorithm can be used to produce a hierarchy of such organizations which we call *summaries*:

For any threshold σ:

1. Let $G_\sigma = (V, E_\sigma)$ where $E_\sigma = \{e : w(e) \geq \sigma\}$.
2. Compute the minimum clique cover of G_σ.
3. Represent each clique by a sequence of representative terms or by any document in the clique.

Fig. 1. The clique-cover algorithm

This algorithm has three nice features. First, by using cliques to cover the similarity graph, we are guaranteed that all the documents in a cluster have the desired degree of similarity. Second, covering the edges of the graph allows vertices to belong to *several* clusters. Documents can be members of multiple clusters, which is a desirable feature when documents have multiple subthemes. Third, this algorithm can be iterated for a range of thresholds, effectively producing a hierarchical organization structure for the information system. Each level in the hierarchy summarizes the collection at a granularity provided by the threshold.

Unfortunately, this approach is computationally intractable. For real corpora, these graphs can be very large. The clique cover problem is NP-complete, and it does not admit polynomial-time approximation algorithms [LY94,Zuc93].

While we cannot perform a clique cover nor even approximate such a cover, we can instead cover our graph by *dense subgraphs*. What we lose in intra-cluster similarity guarantees, we gain in computational efficiency. In the sections that follow, we describe two such covering algorithms and analyze their performance and efficiency.

4.1   Covering with Star-Shaped Subgraphs

While covering the thresholded similarity graph with cliques has many desirable properties as described in the previous section, finding such a covering is, unfortunately, computationally intractable. We shall instead find a clustering of a set of documents by covering the associated thresholded similarity graph with *star-shaped subgraphs*. A star-shaped subgraph on $m + 1$ vertices consists of a single *star center* and m *satellite vertices*, where there exist edges between the star center and each of the satellite vertices. While finding cliques in the thresholded similarity graph G_σ *guarantees* a pairwise similarity between documents of at least σ, it would appear at first glance that finding star-shaped subgraphs in G_σ would provide similarity guarantees between the star center and each of the satellite vertices, but no such similarity guarantees *between satellite vertices*. However, by investigating the geometry of our problem in the vector space model, we can derive a *lower bound* on the similarity between satellite vertices as well as provide a formula for the *expected* similarity between satellite vertices. The latter formula predicts that the pairwise similarity between satellite vertices in a star-shaped subgraph is high, and together with empirical evidence supporting this formula, we shall safely conclude that covering G_σ with star-shaped subgraphs is a reliable method for clustering a set of documents.

Consider three documents C, S_1 and S_2 which are vertices in a star-shaped subgraph of G_σ, where S_1 and S_2 are satellite vertices and C is the star center. By the definition of a star-shaped subgraph of G_σ, we must have that the similarity between C and S_1 is at least σ and that the similarity between C and S_2 is also at least σ. In the vector space model, these similarities are obtained by taking the cosine of the angle between the vectors associated with each document. Let α_1 be the angle between C and S_1, and let α_2 be the angle between C and S_2. We then have that $\cos \alpha_1 \geq \sigma$ and $\cos \alpha_2 \geq \sigma$. Note that the angle between S_1 and S_2 can be at most $\alpha_1 + \alpha_2$, and therefore the similarity between S_1 and S_2 must be at least

$$\cos(\alpha_1 + \alpha_2) = \cos \alpha_1 \cos \alpha_2 - \sin \alpha_1 \sin \alpha_2.$$

Thus, we have a provable lower bound on the similarity between satellite vertices in a star-shaped subgraph of G_σ. If $\sigma = 0.7$, $\cos \alpha_1 = 0.75$ and $\cos \alpha_2 = 0.85$, for instance, we can conclude that the similarity between the two satellite vertices must be at least[3]

$$(0.75) \cdot (0.85) - \sqrt{1 - (0.75)^2}\sqrt{1 - (0.85)^2} \approx 0.29.$$

---

[3] Note that $\sin \theta = \sqrt{1 - \cos^2 \theta}$.

Note that while this may not seem very encouraging, the above analysis is based on absolute worst-case assumptions, and in practice, the similarities between satellite vertices are much higher. We further undertook a study to determine the *expected* similarity between two satellite vertices. By making the mathematical assumption that "similar" documents are essentially "random perturbations" of one another in the vector space model, we were able to derive the following formula for the *expected* similarity between two satellite vertices:

$$\cos \alpha_1 \cos \alpha_2 + \frac{\sigma}{1 + \sigma} \sin \alpha_1 \sin \alpha_2.$$

Note that for the previous example, the above formula would predict a similarity between satellite vertices of approximately 0.78. We have tested this formula against real data, and the results of the test with the MEDLINE data set are shown in Figure 2. In this plot, the x- and y-axes are similarities between cluster centers and satellite vertices, and the z-axis is the actual mean squared prediction error of the above formula for the similarity between satellite vertices. Note that the absolute error (roughly the square root of the mean squared error) is quite small (approximately 0.13 in the worst case), and for reasonably high similarities, the error is negligible. From our tests with real data, we have concluded that this formula is quite accurate, and hence we can conclude that star-shaped subgraphs are reasonably "dense" in the sense that they imply relatively high pairwise similarities between documents.

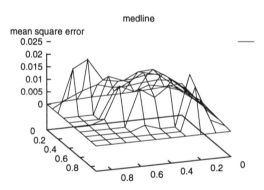

Fig. 2. This figure shows the error for a 6000 abstract subset of MEDLINE.

4.2   The Star and Star+ Algorithm

Motivated by the discussion of the previous section, we now present the *star algorithm* which can be used to organize documents in an information system.

The star algorithm is based on a greedy cover of the thresholded similarity graph by star-shaped subgraphs; the algorithm itself is summarized in Figure 3 below.

For any threshold σ:

1. Let $G_\sigma = (V, E_\sigma)$ where $E_\sigma = \{e : w(e) \geq \sigma\}$.
2. Let each vertex in G_σ initially be *unmarked*.
3. Calculate the degree of each vertex $v \in V$.
4. Let the vertex of highest degree be a star center, and construct a cluster from the star center and its associated satellite vertices. Mark each node in the newly constructed cluster.
5. Set the star center's degree to zero and decrement each satellite vertex's degree by one.
6. Repeat steps 4 and 5 until all nodes are marked.
7. Represent each cluster by the document corresponding to its associated star center.

Fig. 3. The star algorithm

Implemented properly, the star algorithm is very efficient—it can be made to run in time *linear* in the number of edges of the graph, which is $O(N^2)$ where N is the number of vertices in the graph. We will save our discussion of the performance of the star algorithm for the following sections, but as motivation for the subsequent improved algorithm, we will note now that the star algorithm as described above performed very well in a small user study, though somewhat less well on randomly generated data. To improve the performance of the star algorithm, we must improve the "quality" of the clusters it generates. We can improve the quality of the clusters generated by being somewhat more selective about the vertices included in a newly generated cluster. In the augmented *star+ algorithm* described below, a satellite vertex is only included in a cluster if at least one-third of the other candidate satellite vertices have a similarity of at least σ with respect to the satellite vertex in question. (In this heuristic, the parameter "one-third" was arrived at empirically.)

While the star+ algorithm is somewhat slower than the original star algorithm, it produces more accurate clusters, slightly outperforming the star algorithm in a user study and markedly outperforming the star algorithm on randomly generated data. In the sections that follow, we describe our performance analysis of these algorithms in detail.

5   System Description

We have implemented a system for organizing information that uses the star and star+ algorithms. This organization system (that is the basis for the experiments described in this paper) consists of an augmented version of the Smart

For any threshold σ:

1. Let $G_\sigma = (V, E_\sigma)$ where $E_\sigma = \{e : w(e) \geq \sigma\}$.
2. Let each vertex in G_σ initially be *unmarked*.
3. Calculate the degree of each vertex $v \in V$.
4. Let the vertex of highest degree be a star center, and include this vertex in a newly constructed cluster. For each satellite vertex, include the vertex in the cluster if there exist edges incident to this vertex from at least 1/3 of the other satellite vertices. Mark each node in the newly constructed cluster.
5. Set the star center's degree to zero and decrement the degree of each other vertex in the cluster by one.
6. Repeat steps 4 and 5 until all nodes are marked.
7. Represent each cluster by the document corresponding to its associated star center.

Fig. 4. The star+ algorithm

system [Sal91,All95], a user interface we have designed, and an implementation of the star and star+ algorithms on top of Smart. To index the documents we used Smart search engine with a cosine normalization weighting scheme. We enhanced Smart to compute a document to document similarity matrix for a set of retrieved documents or a whole collection. The similarity matrix is used to compute clusters and to visualize the clusters. The user interface is implemented in Tcl/Tk.

The organization system can be run on a whole collection, on a specified subcollection, or on the collection of documents retrieved in response to a user query. Users can input queries by typing in free text. They have the choice of specifying several corpora. This system supports distributed information retrieval but in this paper we do not focus on distribution and we assume only one centrally located corpus. In response to a user query, Smart is invoked to produce a ranked list of the top most relevant documents, their titles, locations and document-to-document similarity information. The similarity information for the entire collection, or for the collection computed by the query engine is provided as input to the star (or star+) algorithm. This algorithm returns a list of clusters and marks their centers.

5.1 Visualization

We developed a visualization method for organized data that presents users with three views of the data (see Figure 5): a list of text titles, a graph that shows the similarity relationship between the documents, and a graph that shows the similarity relationship between the clusters. These views provide users with summaries of the data at different levels of detail: text, document, and topic and facilitate browsing by topic structure.

The connected graph view (inspired by [All95]) has nodes corresponding to the retrieved documents. The nodes are placed in a circle, with nodes corre-

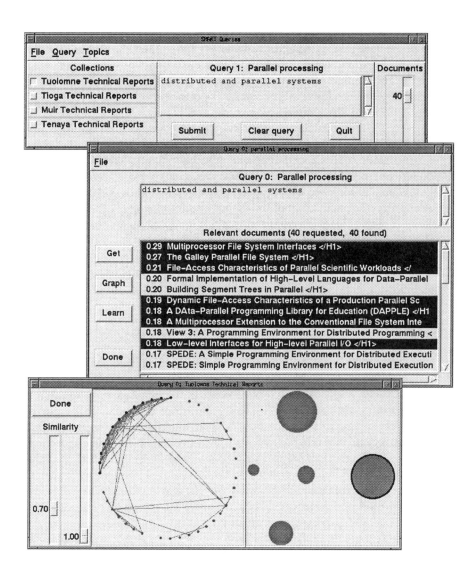

Fig. 5. This is a screen snapshot from a clustering experiment. The top window is the query window. The middle window consists of a ranked list of documents that were retrieved in response to the user query. The user my select "get" to fetch a document or "graph" to request a graphical visualization of the clusters as in the bottom window. The left graph displays all the documents as dots around a circle. Clusters are separated by gaps. The edges denote pairs of documents whose similarity falls between the slider parameters. The right graph displays all the clusters as disks. The radius of a disk is proportional to the size of the cluster. The distance between the disks is proportional to the similarity distance between the clusters.

sponding to the same cluster placed together. Gaps between the nodes allow us to identify clusters easily. Edges between nodes are color coded according to the similarity between the documents. Two slider bars allow the user to establish minimal and maximal weight of edges to be shown.

Another view presents clusters as disks of a size proportional to the size of the corresponding cluster. The distance between two clusters is defined as a distance between the central documents and captures the topic separation between the clusters. Simulated annealing is used to find a cluster placement that minimizes the sum of relative distance errors between clusters. We selected a cooling schedule $\alpha(t) = t/(1 + \beta t)$, where $\beta = 10^{-3}$, initial temperature is 500 and the freezing point is 10^{-2}. This setting provides a good placement when the number of clusters returned by the algorithm is small. This algorithm is fast and its running time does not depend on the number of clusters. When the number of clusters is large, the ellipsoid-based method for Euclidean graph embeddings described in [LLR95] can be used instead.

All three views and a title window allow the user to select an individual document or a cluster. Selection made in one window is simultaneously reflected in the others.

6 Evaluation

Our hypothesis for measuring the performance of a clustering algorithm is that (1) all the different topics should be separated in different clusters, and (2) all the documents relevant to a topic should be aggregated together. We call (1) the *separation* property and (2) the *aggregation* property. The main goal of our experiments is to find whether the star algorithm has good separation and aggregation. A clustering algorithm that guarantees both aggregation and separation is well-suited to improve recall-oriented tasks as well as precision-oriented tasks.

We define three measures, *Precision*, *Recall*, and *critical point* for evaluating the separation and aggregation of our clustering method by drawing inspiration from the precision-recall measures for information retrieval.

Our measures are defined in terms of a "correct" clustering. In the absence of any benchmarks for clustering, we tried to produce one on the MEDLINE collection by using the humanly-assigned indices. We found that if we use the human indices only as a basis for clustering, the resulting clusters do not make sense. This limited our evaluation to relatively small collections (162 documents) that humans could index to produce "correct" clusters, and to randomly generated clustered data. This data in described later in this section.

6.1 Precision-Recall Measures

Precision and Recall for clustering are defined relative to a *correct* clustering of the same data. Let $C_{correct}$ denote the correct clustering of the data and $C_{computed}$ denote the computed clustering. For each document d in the collection we can find the set of clusters $S_{correct} \subset C_{correct}$ and $S_{computed} \subset C_{computed}$ that contain the document. The precision P_d and recall R_d for this document are computed as:

$$P_d = \frac{S_{correct} \cap S_{computed}}{S_{computed}}.$$

$$R_d = \frac{S_{correct} \cap S_{computed}}{S_{correct}}.$$

The precision (respectively, recall) of the clustering algorithm is then computed as the average of the precision (respectively, recall) values for all documents in the corpus:

$$Precision = \frac{\sum_{i=1}^{n} P_{d_i}}{n}.$$

$$Recall = \frac{\sum_{i=1}^{n} R_{d_i}}{n}.$$

Different thresholds for the minimum similarity between two documents in the corpus result in different precision and recall values. If we plot precision and recall against the threshold value we obtain precision and recall curves.

6.2 The Critical Point

Under these measures, a trivial algorithm that clusters each document by itself has high precision but poor recall. A trivial algorithm that clusters all the documents in one cluster has high recall but poor precision. It is easy to produce clustering algorithms that achieve high performance on the recall curve or on the precision curve, but not both. High precision guarantees that different topics are separated in different clusters. High recall guarantees that all the documents relevant to a topic are grouped in the same cluster. We would like to have both good separation between topics and guarantees that all the documents relevant to a topic are aggregated together. We propose a third parameter called the *critical point* as a measure of this idea. The critical point is defined as the intersection point of the precision curve and the recall curve. High critical points guarantee both topic separation and topic aggregation.

6.3 Data Generation

In the absence of any suitable benchmarks by which to test our clustering algorithms, we chose to test our algorithms using data that we either generated or collected ourselves. The data that we used has two forms: first, we generated clustering data randomly in two different ways, and second, we performed a small user study with a real document collection. The former allowed us to have complete control over an arbitrarily large corpus, while the latter allowed us to test against user expectations, albeit for small collections. In the sections that follow, we explain and give the results of our studies with randomly generated data and a real collection of documents.

Generating Random Data Our first experiments involved testing our algorithms against randomly generated clustering data. We generated clustering data by essentially *constructing the similarity graph* for a hypothetical document collection. Our data generation algorithm admitted the following parameters: collection size, mean cluster size and variance, mean cluster overlap and variance, mean intra-cluster edge weight and variance, and mean inter-cluster edge weight and variance. Our procedure for randomly constructing a similarity graph can be divided into two phases: in the first phase, the overlapping clusters of vertices are generated, and in the second phase, appropriate edge weights are generated. To generate the clusters of vertices, a sequence of *cluster size* and *cluster overlap* numbers are generated according to the parameters specified to the algorithm. For example, the following are typical cluster size and cluster overlap sequences:

Cluster size: $24, 12, 22, 29, 16, \ldots$
Cluster overlap: $3, 5, 0, 6, 4, \ldots$

From this data, the proposed clusters can be generated. Cluster 1 would consist of vertices 1 through 24, cluster 2 would consist of vertices 22 through 33, cluster 3 would consist of vertices 29 through 50, and so on—the size of each successive cluster would be dictated by the sequence of cluster sizes, and the overlap between consecutive clusters would be dictated by the sequence of cluster overlaps.

Following the generation of the clusters themselves, all of the edge weights are then constructed. For each pair of vertices, a random edge weight is generated according to either the intra- or inter-cluster distribution, respectively, depending on whether the pair of vertices belong to the same or different clusters. Having generated a similarity graph with known clusters, we can test various algorithms against the known clustering and measure performance according the to the precisions-recall metrics defined above. Note that by carefully setting the mean and variance of the intra- and inter-cluster distributions, one can create similarity graphs with a specified fraction of *faulty data*. If the intra- and inter-cluster distributions *overlap*, then a fraction of the intra-cluster edge weights will look "more like" inter-cluster edge weights, and vice versa. Such a scheme allows one to simulate real, faulty data, and our studies with such randomly generated data are described below.

Experimental Results on Random Data We generated two data sets according to the algorithm described above by varying the percentage of faulty data. The first set has 15% faulty data (that is, overlap between the inter-cluster edges and intr-cluster edges) and the second set has 20% faulty data. We used these clusters as the correct clusters in our precision-recall measures and evaluated the performance of the star and star+ algorithm on this data. The precision-recall curves are shown in Figure 6.

We note that the critical point for the star algorithm is medium at 0.5 for the first data set and 0.38 for the second (more faulty) data set. The critical point of for the star+ algorithm is at 0.9 for the first data set and 0.8 for the second set. We are very encouraged by these high values.

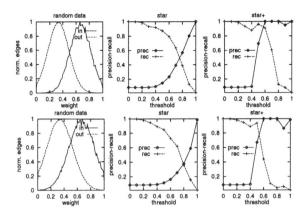

Fig. 6. This figure shows two sets of data. The top set has 15% faulty data and the bottom set has 20% faulty data. For each set we plotted the intra-cluster and inter-cluster edge distribution (left) the precision-recall curves for the star algorithm (middle), and the precision-recall curves for the augmented star algorithm (right).

Generating Random Data on the Sphere While the random data generation procedure described above is very useful in evaluating clustering algorithms, the data created will not necessarily meet the geometric constraints imposed by the vector space model on real data. In this section, we briefly describe a procedure for generating random clustering data which does meet the geometric constraints imposed by the vector space model.

In the vector space model, documents are represented by vectors in a high-dimensional space, and the similarity between pairs of documents is given by the cosine of the angle between the associated vectors. In the previous sections, we described a mechanism for generating the *similarity graph* associated with a collection. In this new data generation procedure, we instead randomly create the *vectors* in high-dimensional space which correspond to documents, and then construct the associated similarity graph from these vectors. In brief, well-spaced *cluster centers* are generated on a unit sphere of high-dimension, and the clusters of documents themselves are generated by randomly perturbing these cluster centers. By carefully varying the "spacing" of the cluster centers as well as the amount of perturbation allowed in generated the cluster documents, we can again allow for a specified overlap of clusters as well as a varying degree of faulty data. Our experiments with this type of randomly generated clustering data are presented below.

Experimental Results on Random Data on the Sphere We generated two data sets according to the algorithm described above by varying the percentage of faulty data. The first set has 7% faulty data (that is, overlap between the inter-cluster edges and intr-cluster edges) and the second set has 12% faulty data. We used these clusters as the correct clusters in our precision-recall measures and evaluated the performance of the star and star+ algorithm on this data. The precision-recall curves are shown in Figure 7.

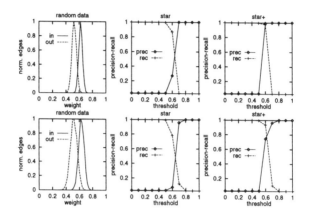

Fig. 7. This figure shows two sets of data. The top set has 7% faulty data and the bottom set has 12% faulty data. For each set we plotted the intra-cluster and inter-cluster edge distribution (left) the precision-recall curves for the star algorithm (middle), and the precision-recall curves for the augmented star algorithm (right).

We note that the critical point for the star algorithm is medium at 0.55 for the first data set and 0.47 for the second (more faulty) data set. The critical point of for the star+ algorithm is at 0.98 for the first data set and 0.8 for the second set. We are very encouraged by these high values. We generated 12 other data sets by varying the probabilities, the distance between the cluster centers, the minimum similarity within a cluster, the number of clusters, and the number of documents per cluster. The locations of the critical points are shown in Fugure 8. The percentage of faulty data seems to be the most sensitive parameter in these experiments.

6.4   A User Study on Technical Reports

We designed an experiment to compute clusters that are "correct" from the perspective of humans, and used these clusters as the correct clusters in the precision-recall computation.

Our study consisted of four graduate students. These students were presented with 162 abstracts from the computer science technical report collection and were only told to cluster the data. No further instructions on how to do the clusters were given. One of the users missed some of the documents so we discarded his data. We then compared the user clusters among themselves and against the star-clustering. The data from this study is shown in Figure 9. The user data is separated in two groups: (a) two users decided to allow one-document clusters

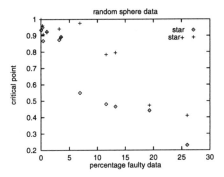

Fig. 8. This figure shows the critical points for 12 experiments with data generated randomly on the sphere.

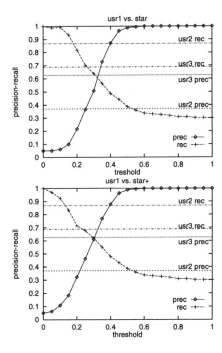

Fig. 9. This figure shows the user-study data for the star and the augmented star algorithm. The plot denoted the precision recall curves achieved by the star+ algorithm against one of user's clusters. The horizontal lines denote the precision and recall values of the other users.

and (b) one user decided to try to cluster all the documents in large clusters. We found that the star algorithm has a high critical point (at 0.6) when compared to the clusters generated by group (a) and a medium critical point (at 0.43) when compared with the clusters generated by group (b). This suggests that the star algorithm has good separation and aggregation of data and is thus well-suited for information organization.

7   Discussion

We have presented and analyzed a clustering algorithm. We have discussed methods for evaluating clustering and for generating benchmarks for clustering. Our user studies present positive evidence that the star clustering algorithm can be used to organize information and further support the cluster hypothesis. Our work extends previous results [HP96] that support using clustering for browsing applications. We argue that by using a clustering algorithm that guarantees the cluster quality through high separation and aggregation, clustering is also beneficial for applications that require high precision.

In the future we hope to do more detailed user studies. In the absence of benchmarks this is a tedious task, as reading and manually organizing thousands of documents is time consuming. We also plan to develop experiments that will address directly the benefits of clustering for retrieval, browsing, and data reduction tasks. Another domain of great interest to us is developing on-line clustering algorithms that will be the basis for self-organizing dynamic information systems.

Acknowledgements

We thank Jonathan Bredin, Mark Montague, and Brian Premore for doing the user study. This work is supported in part by the Navy under contract ONR N00014-95-1-1204 and Rome Labs contract F30602-98-C-0006.

References

[All95] J. Allan. *Automatic hypertext construction*. PhD thesis. Department of Computer Science, Cornell University, January 1995.

[Cro80] W. B. Croft. A model of cluster searching based on classification. *Information Systems*, 5:189-195, 1980.

[Cro77] W. B. Croft. Clustering large files of documents using the single-link method. *Journal of the American Society for Information Science*, pp189-195, November 1977.

[CKP93] D. Cutting, D. Karger, and J. Pedersen. Constant interaction-time scatter/gather browsing of very large document collections. In *Proceedings of the 16th SIGIR*, 1993.

[HP96] M. Hearst and J. Pedersen. Reexamining the cluster hypothesis: Scatter/Gather on Retrieval Results. In *Proceedings of the 19th SIGIR*, 1996.

[JD88] A. Jain and R. Dubes. *Algorithms for Clustering Data*, Prentice Hall 1988.

[JR71] N. Jardine and C.J. van Rijsbergen. The use of hierarchical clustering in information retrieval, 7:217-240, 1971.

[KP93] G. Kortsarz and D. Peleg. On choosing a dense subgraph. In *Proceedings of the 34th Annual Symposium on Foundations of Computer Science (FOCS)*, 1993.

[LC96] A. Leouski and B. Croft. An evaluation of techniques for clustering search results. Technical report, Department of Computer Science, the University of Massachusetts at Amherst, 1996.

[LLR95] N. Linial, E. London, and Y. Rabinovich. The geometry of graphs and some of its algorithmic applications. *Combinatorica* 15(2):215-245, 1995.

[LY94] C. Lund and M. Yannakakis. On the hardness of approximating minimization problems. *Journal of the ACM* 41, 960–981, 1994.

[Rij79] C.J. van Rijsbergen. *Information Retrieval*. Butterworths, London, 1979.

[RA95] D. Rus and J. Allan. Structural queries in electronic corpora. In *Proceedings of DAGS95: Electronic Publishing and the Information Superhighway*, May 1995.

[Sal89] G. Salton. *Automatic Text Processing: the transformation, analysis, and retrieval of information by computer*, Addison-Wesley, 1989.

[Sal91] G. Salton. The Smart document retrieval project. In *Proceedings of the Fourteenth Annual International ACM/SIGIR Conference on Research and Development in Information Retrieval*, pages 356-358.

[SM83] G. Salton and M. McGill. *Introduction to Modern Information Retrieval*. McGraw-Hill, New York, 1983.

[SA93] G. Salton and J. Allan. Selective text utilization and text traversal. In *Hypertext '93 Proceedings*, pages 131-144, Seattle, Washington, 1993.

[SJJ70] K. Spark Jones and D. Jackson. The use of automatically-obtained keyword classifications for information retrieval. *Inform. Stor. Retr.* 5:174-201, 1970.

[Tur90] H. Turtle. Inference networks for document retrieval. PhD thesis. University of Massachusetts, Amherst, 1990.

[VGJ95] E. Voorhees, N. Gupta, and B. Johnson-Laird. Learning collection fusion strategies. In *Proceedings of the 18th SIGIR*, Seattle, WA, 1995.

[Voo85] E. Voorhees. The cluster hypothesis revisited. In *Proceedings of the 8th SIGIR*, pp 95-104, 1985.

[Wil88] P. Willett. Recent trends in hierarchical document clustering: A critical review. *Information Processing and Management*, 24:(5):577-597, 1988.

[Wor71] S. Worona. Query clustering in a large document space. In Ed. G. Salton, *The SMART Retrieval System*, pp 298-310. Prentice-Hall, 1971.

[Zuc93] D. Zuckerman. NP-complete problems have a version that's hard to approximate. In *Proceedings of the Eight Annual Structure in Complexity Theory Conference*, IEEE Computer Society, 305–312, 1993.

On the Specification of the Display of Documents in Multi-lingual Computing

Myatav Erdenechimeg, Richard Moore, and Yumbayar Namsrai*

United Nations University, International Institute for Software Technology,
P.O. Box 3058, Macau
E-mail: {me,rm,ny}@iist.unu.edu

Abstract. The first phase of UNU/IIST's MultiScript project comprised a comprehensive study and analysis of multi-lingual documents, on the basis of which a formal model of a generic multi-directional, multi-lingual document was developed [1, 2, 4] using the RAISE specification language RSL [8]. We briefly review this formal model, then investigate the requirements on the physical properties of the character sets used to display and print multi-directional, multi-lingual documents and extend the model and the formal specification appropriately. This reveals that although the alignment information contained in the character sets which are currently in common use is perfectly sufficient for displaying and printing documents in which the text is unidirectional, there is typically a shortcoming as far as multi-directional texts are concerned which means that it is impossible to specify the alignment of characters from a horizontal script with characters from a vertical script other than by choosing some arbitrary default or by specifying the alignment on an instance by instance basis. We propose a simple extension to the alignment information of a character set to alleviate this problem and formally specify its properties.

1 Introduction

Broadly speaking, the majority of the world's scripts can be categorised into four main groups according to the direction in which they are read and written. We call these groups the "HL", "HR", "VL" and "VR" groups. Scripts in the HL group are written horizontally from left to right, with lines of text proceeding downwards, and include Latin, Greek, Cyrillic, Thai, and Bengali; those in the HR group are written horizontally from right to left, also with lines of text proceeding downwards, and include Arabic and Hebrew; those in the VL group are written vertically downwards in columns, the columns proceeding from left to right, and include traditional Mongolian script as well as related scripts like

---

* This work was done while the author was on leave of absence from the Department of Computer Science, Mathematics Faculty, The National University of Mongolia, Ulaanbaatar, Mongolia. He is now at the Department of Software Engineering, Computer Science and Management Institute, Mongolian Technical University, Ulaanbaatar, Mongolia; email: ny@csms.edu.mn

Manchu and Todo; and those in the VR group are written vertically downwards, with the columns proceeding from right to left, and include Japanese, Chinese and Korean.

However, despite this diversity in reading and writing direction, software systems which process multi-lingual documents typically tend to be unidirectional. Most commonly they impose the horizontal left-to-right directionality of the HL group, although some systems, particularly those which have primarily been produced to support a script which does not belong to this HL group, do adopt the natural directionality of that script and some indeed allow the user to change the reading and writing direction, though generally they neither allow this direction to change within a document nor support all four of the main reading and writing directions.

In [4] we present a generic abstract model of multi-lingual documents which not only allows the overall reading and writing direction of the whole document to be defined but which also allows different parts of the document to have different reading and writing directions. We also give a formal specification of this basic abstract model in RSL, the RAISE specification language [8].

That work represents part of the results of the second phase of UNU/IIST's MultiScript project, and extends and slightly modifies a preliminary model which was developed following a comprehensive study and analysis of multi-lingual documents during the first phase of the project [1, 2]. We briefly review the salient points of this basic model and its formal specification in Section 2.

The present paper extends this model to include information which is necessary to define how these multi-directional, multi-lingual documents are displayed and printed. On the basis of this, it proposes an extension to the information related to a font which would allow a character from a font for a vertical script to be aligned automatically with a character from a font for a horizontal script without rotating one of the characters.

2   The Basic Model of Multi-lingual Documents

The fundamental building block in the model is a *frame*, which represents a piece of text which is read and written in a single direction. This direction is defined by the *orientation* of the frame, which in turn is determined by its *entry point* and its *line stream*.

The entry point simply defines the position at which reading or writing within the frame begins, and is situated at the top left-hand corner of the frame for the HL and VL groups of scripts and at the top right-hand corner of the frame for the HR and VR groups. The line stream defines the direction in which the text within the frame is read or written and is horizontal for the HL and HR groups of scripts and vertical for the VL and VR groups. Consecutive lines[1] of text are aligned perpendicular to the line stream and proceed away from the entry point, so that for horizontal line stream they proceed downwards if the entry point is

---

[1] Lines may be either horizontal or vertical.

at the top and upwards if it is at the bottom, while for vertical line stream they proceed to the right if the entry point is at the left and to the left if it is at the right.

The string of text within a frame effectively consists of a sequence of characters, although this is actually divided into substrings to allow for the fact that things like the typeface and the size of the characters might change without changing the orientation. Each of these substrings is a piece of *formatted text*. A frame may also contain other frames, possibly with different reading and writing directions. These may either be embedded within the text of the frame (so that when the contents of the frame are displayed their position is determined entirely by the text preceding them) or may be positioned freely and independently (like the articles in a newspaper). We refer to frames in this latter category as *free frames*.

In the formal RSL model, we represent frames using the *record* type 'Frame'. This comprises the three components of a frame: its orientation, represented by the type 'Orientation'; the string of text it contains, represented as a list of pieces of formatted text, each piece being represented by the type 'FormattedText'; and its free frames, represented as a list of *frame identifiers* (references, or pointers, to frames; the type 'FrameId'). The string and the free frames together constitute the contents of the frame.

> **type**
>> Frame ::
>>> orient : Orientation
>>> string : FormattedText*
>>> freeFrames : FrameId*

Both orientation and formatted text are also defined as record types. The type 'Orientation' comprises an entry point and a line stream, which are both defined using *variant* types which simply enumerate all possible values of those types. The type 'FormattedText' consists of some formatting information (the type 'FormatInfo') and a list of *tokens*. A token is either a character or a frame identifier, as represented by the *union* type, the frame identifier being used to model the case in which a piece of text contains an embedded frame with different orientation.

Formatting information and characters are defined only as abstract types or *sorts*. Thus, for example, the type 'FormatInfo' represents the (at this level unspecified) formatting information associated with a piece of formatted text. This might include, for instance, the typeface and the size of the characters.

> **type**
>> Orientation :: entry : Entry_Point stream : Line_Stream,
>> Entry_Point == left | right,
>> Line_Stream == horizontal | vertical,
>> FormattedText :: format : FormatInfo chars : Token*,
>> Token = Character | FrameId,
>> FormatInfo,
>> Character

With this model of frames, a document as a whole can essentially be considered simply as a single frame, the orientation of that frame determining the sense in which the document should be read and the contents of the frame (both the string, which may of course contain embedded subframes, and the free frames) representing the text within the document. We call this frame the *root* of the document.

In the formal model the root is represented as a frame identifier, and the contents of the document is recorded frame by frame in the *frame map* which relates each frame identifier appearing in the document to an actual frame. Our model of a document also includes the notion of hyperlink references from some part of a document to some other part of the same document or to some part of some other document. In fact we generalise this further and consider documents to be collected together into libraries, the hyperlinks then allowing references from one document to another which may be in a different library.

We therefore define a type 'Doc' as a record type containing three fields, one for each of the components mentioned above. Both the frame map and the hyperlinks are represented as *map* types. The frame map links frame identifiers to frames, and the hyperlinks associates frame identifiers in the current document with other frame identifiers, the documents to which those other frames belong and the libraries to which those documents belong being indicated respectively by the *document identifier* (represented by the abstract type 'DocId') and *library identifier* (represented by the abstract type 'LibId') components of the *product* type in the range of the map.

type
    Doc ::
        root : FrameId
        frame_map : FrameId $\overrightarrow{m}$ Frame
        hyper_links : FrameId $\overrightarrow{m}$ (LibId × DocId × FrameId),
    FrameId,
    DocId,
    LibId

The document identifier distinguishes individual documents in a library, and a library is then simply represented using a map type from document identifiers to documents. Similarly, the library identifier distinguishes individual libraries within the whole collection of libraries, represented by the type 'Libraries' which is again a map type.

type
$\quad$ Library = DocId $\twoheadrightarrow$ Document,
$\quad$ Libraries = LibId $\twoheadrightarrow$ Library

In order for the record type 'Doc' to represent only valid or well-formed documents, its fields must satisfy various consistency conditions as follows:

1. the root of the document must occur in the domain of the frame map in order for the contents of the document to be defined;
2. the frame map must be non-circular to ensure that the contents of the document are finite. This is equivalent to the condition that no frame of the document should be contained in (a subframe of) itself;
3. any frame identifier which is defined as the source of some hyperlink in the document must belong to the document;
4. the frame map of the document must record all frames belonging to the document, including the root frame, and no others;
5. each frame in the document must have a unique identifier, that is a given frame identifier cannot appear in the contents of two different frames in the document. This is to ensure that it is possible to distinguish two frames in the document which have the same contents, for example when editing the document.

We formalise these properties in the Boolean-valued function 'is_wf_document', and valid documents are then represented by the type 'Document' which is defined as a *subtype* of the type 'Doc' comprising only those values which satisfy the consistency condition.

value
$\quad$ is_wf_document : Doc $\rightarrow$ **Bool**
$\quad$ is_wf_document(d) $\equiv$
$\quad\quad$ **let** mk_Doc(r, fm, hm) = d **in**
$\quad\quad\quad$ r $\in$ **dom** fm $\wedge$
$\quad\quad\quad$ is_non_circular(fm) $\wedge$
$\quad\quad\quad$ **dom** hm $\subseteq$ **dom** fm $\wedge$
$\quad\quad\quad$ **let** id_list = all_frames(r, fm) **in**
$\quad\quad\quad\quad$ is_non_repeating(id_list) $\wedge$ (**elems** id_list = **dom** fm \ {r})
$\quad\quad\quad$ **end**
$\quad\quad$ **end**

type $\quad$ Document = {| d : Doc • is_wf_document(d) |}

The definitions of the three auxiliary functions 'is_non_circular', 'all_frames' and 'is_non_repeating' which are used in the definition of 'is_wf_document' are omitted here for brevity but can be found in [4].

$\quad$ It is worth noting at this point that there is some similarity between the model of a document in terms of frames and formatted text which we have presented above and the layout view of a document within the ODA standard (see for example [7]), which uses pages, frames, blocks and contents. However, our model is intended not as a layout view but as a structural (or logical) view of a document.

As such, we believe it to be entirely compatible with, and indeed an abstraction of, the logical view of a document in ODA. In this abstraction, each element of the logical view of a document in ODA (for example the *title*, the *abstract*, the *body*, etc.) would be represented as a frame, with subframes being used to represent the (inclusion) relationship between these entities. Then the textual contents of each entity would be simply the contents of these frames, possibly itself with embedded subframes and free frames to represent changes in directionality of the text or other structuring.

For example, a document having a title, one author, an abstract, and a body could be represented in our model as a document in which the root frame contains four subframes, one for each of the above components, and no free frames or text. Then the *author* frame could contain simply two subframes, one for the author's name and one for the institute; the *abstract* frame would contain simply the text of the abstract (which may perhaps contain subframes or free frames); and so on. In this way, structure such as that defined in the logical view in ODA is represented in our model by defining at the topmost level a corresponding structure constructed only of frames and subframes, and the contents of the lowest level subframes in this structure then represent the actual textual contents of the document.

3   Properties of Characters

We now go on to consider the layout of the contents of a document. This will depend on the size of the characters used within its text, which is determined by the font in which the characters are to be printed. We assume the font, or at least its name, will be obtainable from the formatting information within each piece of formatted text.

> **type**   Font
> **value**   font : FormatInfo → Font

In a typical font used in computer-based text processing systems (see for example [5]), the characters and symbols, which often come from a single script or family of scripts, are each drawn inside a rectangle of a fixed height, generally in such a way that the characters are correctly positioned to form a line of text if their containing rectangles are aligned with each other. The default horizontal spacing between characters obtained by aligning the characters in this way can be altered by the insertion of spacing characters (called *kerns*), which may have either positive or negative width, negative kerns having the effect of moving characters closer together than normal. However, characters from different fonts may have different heights, and lining these up using only the bounding rectangle is unlikely to produce the desired result: the smaller characters are displayed either too high or too low as illustrated in Figure 1.

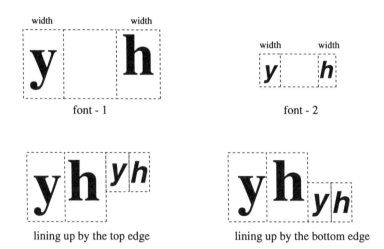

Fig. 1. Aligning Characters using the Bounding Rectangle

Each character in a font therefore includes an extra piece of alignment information, called its *baseline*, which defines how it is to be aligned against characters with different heights. For a font supporting characters from a horizontal script this baseline takes the form of a horizontal line dividing the character's bounding rectangle into two rectangles, and the vertical dimension of the rectangle above the baseline is then called the *height* of the character while the vertical dimension of the rectangle below the baseline is called its *depth*. Characters from different fonts (or indeed from the same font) are then aligned correctly if their baselines form a continuous line. This is illustrated in Figure 2. For vertical scripts the situation is analogous except that the baseline divides the character vertically.

This alignment information is perfectly adequate if all the characters in a line of text have the same orientation, irrespective of whether the line of text is horizontal or vertical. However, if we wish to embed characters from a vertical script in a horizontal script or vice versa, then we can only line up the characters using the baselines if we first rotate the embedded characters, because otherwise the baselines are perpendicular to each other.

This rotation is typically done in such a way that the rotated characters have the "correct" orientation with respect to the line stream of the text in which they are embedded, that is if we rotate the page to make the enforced line stream match the natural one of the embedded characters then the embedded characters appear normal.

This is illustrated in the top and bottom examples in Figure 3. The first of these shows standard English text in which Mongolian characters, normally written vertically, are embedded. The Mongolian characters have been rotated through 90° anticlockwise (so if we rotate the page through 90° clockwise the Mongolian characters will appear in their normal orientation). The bottom ex-

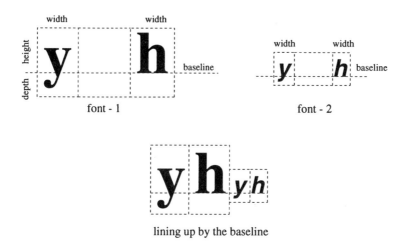

Fig. 2. Aligning Characters using the Baseline

ample shows Chinese text written in its traditional orientation (vertically top to bottom with the columns progressing from right to left) in which English text is embedded. In this case the characters of the English text have been rotated through 90° clockwise (and rotating the page through 90° anticlockwise makes the English text appear in its normal orientation). In the middle example, which shows Arabic text embedded in English text, the Arabic characters are not rotated but are simply read from right to left as they would normally be.

To allow characters with different orientations to be aligned automatically, we therefore propose an extension to the alignment information stored in the font, namely that each character in the font should have two baselines, one horizontal and one vertical.

In the formal specification, we define a type 'DisplayChar' which represents the physical character as it will be printed, and a function 'font_characters' which extracts the display forms of the characters in a font in terms of their codes (the type 'Character'). A given character is printable in a font if a display character for it can be found in that font, and each font should contain at least one printable character (this property is stated in the axiom below).

type   DisplayChar

value
    font_characters : Font → (Character $\rightarrow$ DisplayChar),

    is_printable : Character × Font → **Bool**
    is_printable(ch, f) ≡ ch ∈ **dom** font_characters(f)

axiom   ∀ f : Font • font_characters(f) ≠ [ ]

```
For  example  you can see on the chart the forms of a letter
"a"  at the beginning  ᵀᵀ (code  is  64); in the middle   ᵣ (96)
(common),  ᵣ ( 128  ( in the case of ᎤᎶ );  at  the  end  it has  3
different  forms   ⁊ (160),   ʃ ( 192)   ᨦ(224)   ( in the case
of  ᎷᏣ⁊⹐ᏒᏒᏥ⹐ Ꭴ⁊ ⹐⹐ )
```

(a)

The words الإسلام and العرب mean Islam and the Arabs.
The words الإسلام و العرب mean Islam and the Arabs.

(b)

(c)

Fig. 3. Examples of Multi-lingual Documents

The size of a (printable) character is then made up of four components: *left width*, *right width*, *height* and *depth*. The axiom below ensures that all printable characters in a font have well-defined size.

type   ElemSize = Width × Width × Height × Height

value   size : Character × Font $\xrightarrow{\sim}$ ElemSize

axiom
 [definedness]
  ∀ ch : Character, f : Font •
   size(ch, f) **post true pre** is_printable(ch, f)

Rotating a (display) character is then straightforward. We define a type 'Rotation', which defines rotations as a multiple of 90°, and assume that the rotation of the characters is part of the formatting information associated with a piece of formatted text.

type Rotation = {| r : **Nat** • r ≤ 3 |}

value rotation : FormatInfo → Rotation

We then define a function 'rotate', which rotates a display character through 90°, and a function 'display' which returns the display character associated with a given character from a given font rotated by some given amount.

value
 rotate : DisplayChar → DisplayChar,

 display : Character × Font × Rotation $\xrightarrow{\sim}$ DisplayChar
 display(ch, f, r) ≡ **if** r = 0 **then** font_characters(f)(ch)
  else rotate(display(ch, f, r − 1)) **end**
  pre is_printable(ch, f)

The size of a rotated display character is defined by the axiom 'size_rotate' below. This is written in terms of a derived function 'size' on display characters which, for printable characters from a font, coincides with the function of the same name defined above. This rotation is illustrated in Figure 4.

value size : DisplayChar → ElemSize

axiom
 [size_font_characters]
  ∀ ch : Character, f : Font •
   size(font_characters(f)(ch)) ≡ size(ch, f)
    pre is_printable(ch, f),

[size_rotate]
  ∀ ch : DisplayChar •
    size(rotate(ch)) ≡
      let (lw, rw, h, d) = size(ch) **in** (d, h, lw, rw) **end**

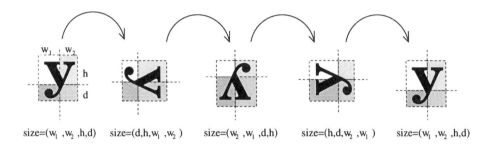

size=(w₁ ,w₂ ,h,d)   size=(d,h,w₁ ,w₂)   size=(w₂ ,w₁ ,d,h)   size=(h,d,w₂ ,w₁)   size=(w₁ ,w₂ ,h,d)

Fig. 4. Rotating a Display Character

We next introduce kerns by introducing a type 'ExtendedChar' which includes both display characters and kerns. We assign a single size to a kern as is
normal, but consider this as being two dimensional instead of single dimensional.
This allows us to use kerns in both vertical and horizontal text interchangeably.

    type
    ExtendedChar == view_char(char : DisplayChar) | kern(wdth : Width)

    value
        size : ExtendedChar → ElemSize
          size(v) ≡
               case v **of**
                  view_char(ch) → size(ch),
                  _ → **let** wd = wdth(v) **in** (wd, zero, wd, zero) **end**
               end

The model has been extended further to include definitions and specifications
of words, lines, etc. as well as of how documents can be created and edited. Full
details of these extensions can be found in [6, 3].

4 Conclusions

We have described a simple model of multi-lingual documents in which different
parts of the document can have different reading and writing directions, and we
have given a formal specification of this in RSL. We have also given the first

part of a specification of how the characters, words and lines of such a document can be determined, and have proposed a simple extension to the alignment information associated with fonts to allow both the rotation of characters and the relative positioning of characters from horizontal and vertical scripts to be easily and automatically defined.

The work reported here represents part of the output of the second phase of UNU/IIST's 'MultiScript' project, full details of which can be found in [4, 6, 3]. In the third phase of the project we intend to implement a demonstrator system based on this work.

References

1. Myatav Erdenechimeg and Richard Moore. Multi-directional Multi-lingual Script Processing. Technical Report 75, UNU/IIST, P.O.Box 3058, Macau, June 1996.
2. Myatav Erdenechimeg and Richard Moore. Multi-directional Multi-lingual Script Processing. In *Proceedings of the Seventeenth International Conference on the Computer Processing of Oriental Languages, Vol. 1*, pages 29 – 34. Oriental Languages Computer Society, Inc., 1997.
3. Myatav Erdenechimeg and Richard Moore. MultiScript III: Creating and Editing Multi-lingual Documents. Technical Report 113, UNU/IIST, P.O.Box 3058, Macau, September 1997.
4. Myatav Erdenechimeg, Richard Moore, and Yumbayar Namsrai. MultiScript I: The Basic Model of Multi-lingual Documents. Technical Report 105, UNU/IIST, P.O.Box 3058, Macau, June 1997.
5. Donald E. Knuth. *The TEX Book*. Addison-Wesley Publishing Company, 1984.
6. Yumbayar Namsrai and Richard Moore. MultiScript II: Displaying and Printing Multi-lingual Documents. Technical Report 112, UNU/IIST, P.O.Box 3058, Macau, June 1997.
7. Charles Nicholas and Lawrence Welsch. On the Interchangeability of SGML and ODA/ODIF. *Electronic Publishing - Origination, Dissemination and Design*, 5(3):105–131, September 1992.
8. The RAISE Language Group. *The RAISE Specification Language*. BCS Practitioner Series. Prentice Hall, 1992.

Spotting Topics with the Singular Value Decomposition *

Charles Nicholas[1] and Randall Dahlberg[2]

[1] University of Maryland Baltimore County
[2] U.S. Department of Defense

Abstract. The singular value decomposition, or SVD , has been studied in the past as a tool for detecting and understanding patterns in a collection of documents. We show how the matrices produced by the SVD calculation can be interpreted, allowing us to spot patterns of characters that indicate particular topics in a corpus. A test collection, consisting of two days of AP newswire traffic, is used as a running example.

1 Introduction

We address the question of how to analyze a large collection of documents to see what topics are discussed (or perhaps just mentioned) in that collection. We assume that the collection is large, perhaps on the order of hundreds of megabytes of text or more. The documents may have been written by many people, perhaps in different languages. New documents may be added to the collection at any time, and we will not know in advance exactly which topics occur in the collection.

We assume that a "topic" can be characterized by some set of words or phrases, which by themselves may carry little meaning, but when appearing together imply that the given topic is indeed being discussed. One obvious way to approach this problem is to create a set of "standard" queries, designed to search on those words or phrases that characterize the given topic. Although this technique may be effective in some cases, it will be slow for large collections, and it won't tell us when new topics arise. We therefore need a technique that lets us analyze the entire collection (or better still, that portion of it which has been added since the last analysis) to see what topics are present, whether we know of those topics beforehand or not. We present a technique for doing this, based on the singular value decomposition. Section 2 describes the SVD . Section 3 explains how useful results can be obtained without computing the full SVD . Section 4 describes how the output of the SVD can be interpreted. We summarize related work in Section 5.

---

* Contact author: Charles Nicholas, Department of Computer Science and Electrical Engineering, UMBC, 1000 Hilltop Circle, Baltimore, MD 21250 USA, 410-455-2594, -3969 (fax), nicholas@cs.umbc.edu

2   The Singular Value Decomposition

We work with a *term-document matrix*, in which entry $f_{i,j}$ is the number of times term i occurs in document j. Throughout this paper, we will use an example term-document matrix constructed from two days of Associated Press newswire text. The text consists of 225 news stories (in English) from January 1 and January 2 of 1989. The documents are marked up in accordance with the SGML document type definition supplied by the TREC project.

The terms, corresponding to rows in the term-document matrix, are n-grams made up of characters from the document [3]. We chose $n = 5$, so characters 1-5 make up the first n-gram , characters 2-6 make up the second n-gram , and so forth. There are many strings of length n in this corpus, if one considers all possible sequences of characters, but relatively few of these n-grams ever occur in English, and fewer still, only 96841, n-grams actually occur in the test corpus. (Only the text portions of the documents were used; header information and SGML markup was filtered out before the n-gram processing.)

Since there are 225 documents in the test corpus, its term-document matrix is of dimension 96841 × 225. Some n-grams occur in many documents, i.e. n-grams that correspond to "stop words". Apart from these n-grams , however, most n-grams occur in only a small percentage of the documents, which implies that most entries in a given column of the term-document matrix are zero. Therefore, most of the entries in the matrix are zero, and the matrix is considered sparse. This is important, because we will use algorithms that work especially well (in terms of both execution time and memory requirements) on sparse matrices. In general, the sparser the matrix the better, since only the non-zero entries in the matrix are worked with.

Recall that each column of A represents a document, where the entries in each row is the number of times the corresponding n-gram occurs in that document. In the AP matrix, for example, each document is represented as a vector in a high-dimensional space, namely R^{96841}. The SVD computes three matrices U, Σ and V such that the $m \times n$ term-document matrix A, of rank r, can be expressed as their product, i.e.

$$A = U \times \Sigma \times V^T$$

where U is an $m \times m$ orthogonal matrix; Σ is the $m \times n$ diagonal matrix in which the singular values of A are listed, in descending order, from the upper-left corner; and V is an $n \times n$ orthogonal matrix. The number of nonzero singular values produced is the same as the rank of the original matrix. Since the rank of A is r, we may replace U by the result of truncating its last $m - r$ columns, replace V by the result of truncating the last $n - r$ columns, and replace Σ by the result of truncating the last $m - r$ of its rows and the last $n - r$ of its columns. In the AP example, where the number of terms far exceeds the number of documents, the rank of A is the number of distinct documents in the corpus. (Note that in this sense, a document that is a duplicate of another document, or made up by concatenating one document with another, is not distinct.) In larger collections, the number of documents may exceed the number of terms.

The columns of U can be thought of as "term" vectors, in the sense that each column of U represents a linear combination, or pattern, of n-grams that tend to occur in documents in the same proportion. (Note that each n-gram must participate in at least one such linear combination, but may participate in several of them. The entry in any column, i.e. the coefficient for that n-gram in the corresponding linear combination, may be positive or negative.) By construction, the columns of U are orthonormal, i.e. orthogonal and of length 1. The number of columns in U is the rank r of the original matrix A. Orthogonality implies that the columns of U span a vector space of dimension r, and can therefore be regarded as axes in that space.

The matrix Σ is the diagonal matrix formed by the singular values of A, in descending order. (The singular values of the matrix A are the nonnegative square roots of the eigenvalues of the matrix AA^T or $A^T A$.) The singular values (along with the entries in the matrix V) indicate how important the different "term" vectors are in each document, and those same singular values (and the entries in the matrix U) indicate how much each document contributes to the corpus.

It can be shown that the first r columns of U form an orthonormal basis for the space spanned by the columns of A, i.e. the document space and the coordinates of the document vectors with respect to this basis are simply the rows of the matrix ΣV^T. Similarly, the rows of V^T form an orthonormal basis for the space spanned by the rows of A, i.e. the term space and the coordinates of the term vectors with respect to this basis are the rows of the matrix $U\Sigma$. The matrix Σ provides scaling, in the sense that for any row i of the "scaled" matrix $S = \Sigma V^T$, each entry $S_{i,j}$ in row i of S is the coordinate of document j along the axis determined by the ith column, U_i, of the matrix U. If the columns of U are regarded as axes of the document space, then each axis somehow represents whatever it is that makes that document unique. Indeed, what makes a document unique is that at least one n-gram occurs in that document in different proportion than in any other document in the corpus.

So each document can be plotted against the different term vectors, and each term can be plotted against the different document vectors. The fact that the first r columns of U and the topmost r rows of V^T span the same space introduces a duality that we will exploit in order to better understand the structure of the corpus.

3   Approximating the SVD

The SVD is a standard feature of symbolic computation packages such as MAT-LAB, and specialized SVD software is available. Berry's SVDPACK contains several algorithms for calculating the SVD , optimized for supercomputers [1]. However, the full SVD algorithm is $O(n^3)$ in time complexity, where n is the number of entries in A. Sparse matrix versions of the SVD are available in both MATLAB and SVDPACK, but these are still $O(n^3)$ in the number of non-zero entries in A. In the AP example, the 96841×225 term-document matrix A

has 427,432 non-zero entries. SVDPACK took about five and a half minutes to compute the full SVD of this matrix. [1]

Since many interesting corpora are much larger than the AP example, it is important to note that useful results can be obtained without computing the full SVD . The dyadic decomposition of the matrix A is given by

$$A = \sum_{i=1}^{r} u_i \cdot \sigma_i \cdot v_i^T$$

and it can be shown that for integer k, $1 \le k \le r$,

$$A_k = \sum_{i=1}^{k} u_i \cdot \sigma_i \cdot v_i^T$$

is the closest rank-k matrix to A [2]. In other words, by choosing to compute only the first k so-called singular triplets u_i, σ_i, v_i^T, we can capture as much of the information in A as we wish. MATLAB and SVDPACK both allow the user to specify k in this manner: For example, the MATLAB command to compute the SVD using the first 15 singular triplets would be

```
>> [u,s,v] = svds(A,15);
```

Computing this SVD , for the relatively small AP test corpus, took MATLAB about 11 minutes for $k = 5$, almost 22 minutes for $k = 10$, and 68 minutes for $k = 15$. SVDPACK is much faster; as noted above, the full SVD on the test corpus (i.e. $k = 225$) took less than six minutes.

The cost of the SVD calculation for a large collection raises the question of how to choose n as well as k so that computation is minimized but little or no interesting information is lost. With a relatively small corpus, such as the AP data used in this paper, the term-document matrix is of manageable size, and the SVD calculation takes just a few minutes using SVDPACK. With larger corpora, the size of the matrix becomes an issue.

The choice of n, i.e. the length of the n-grams to be used, is the first major decision. The larger the value of n, the more terms there will be; the number of n-grams roughly doubles with each increment of n. In the 225 document AP corpus, for example, there are 42316 n-grams when $n = 4$, 96841 n-grams when $n = 5$, and 162993 n-grams when $n = 6$. Since the number of terms determines the size of the term-document matrix for a fixed set of documents, it behooves us to use the smallest suitable n. We have used $n = 5$ in most of our research, since in our experience lower values of n don't capture topic information well enough. There is evidence to support the claim that shorter n-grams are sufficient for spotting differences in language or writing style [7].

Once n has been chosen, the corpus can be read, and the term-document matrix constructed. It is possible to column-normalize the matrix at this point,

[1] We used SVDPACK and MATLAB (version 5.0) running on Sun Ultra 1 workstations with 192MB of memory.

in order to compensate for different document lengths, and we did that in several experiments. However, we found that the column-normalized matrix was no more useful at spotting topics, so we focused our attention on other parts of the process. Once the term-document matrix is built, a term-weighting strategy may reduce the number of non-zero entries in the matrix, and may reduce the number of terms. We used the log-entropy term-weighting used by Dumais [5]. After calculating the term weights, we plotted the non-zero values, and chose a threshold of 0.5. Entries in the matrix below this threshold were mapped to zero. The number of terms was reduced by 7100, from 96841 down to 89741, a reduction of about 7%. Although many values in the matrix were mapped to zero, no document had all of its entries mapped to zero, so no documents were lost.

The rest of the paper uses the two day AP test corpus, with log-entropy term weighting applied, and weighted term frequencies less than 0.5 mapped to zero. The SVD of this matrix was calculated, and a plot of the first 15 singular values is shown in Figure 1.

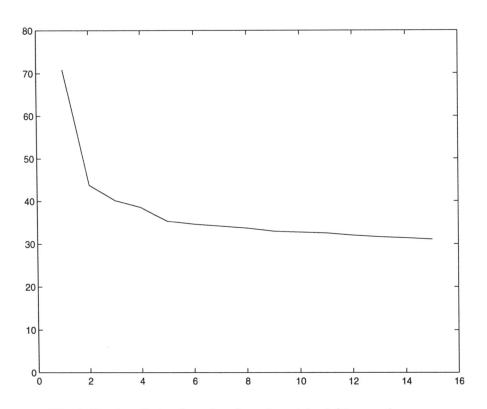

Fig. 1. The first 15 singular values from the weighted AP example corpus.

Considering Figure 1, it is obvious that the first singular value is much larger than the others. (Recall that these singular values are the first entries on the main diagonal of Σ, so by construction the other $rank(A) - 15$ singular values are smaller than those shown here.) The singular values themselves don't support deep interpretation. However, the fact that there is a sharp drop from the first singular value to the second indicates that the corpus is relatively homogeneous. If the corpus was made up of several different sub-collections, written in sharply different styles or vocabularies, then there would be several singular values, one or more for each sub-collection, that together explain some part of the variance within the corpus.

In a multi-lingual corpus, the first few columns of U represent the common n-grams (i.e. stopwords) for the different languages. We subjected another corpus, containing Russian, French, Danish and Norwegian text, to similar analysis. No one singular value dominated, as it did in the AP corpus. Instead, there were four roughly comparable values, all relatively large when compared to the other singular values (see Figure 2).

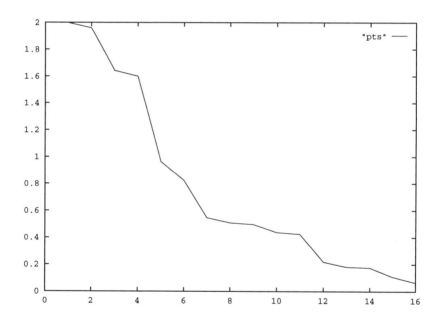

Fig. 2. The singular values from the column normalized multilingual corpus.

The first term vector contained common Russian n-grams , and the second contained French n-grams . The third term vector was again Russian, but the fourth was a mixture of Norwegian and Danish. Two singular triples were needed to "explain" the variance introduced by the Russian text, since that material was so different from the rest. On the other hand, since the Danish and Norwegian languages are so similar, only one singular triple was needed to explain the bulk of the variance introduced by those portions of the corpus written in either of those languages.

4   Interpretation of Singular Vectors

Recall that the columns of the matrix U, also known as the "left" singular vectors, represent linear combinations of n-grams that tend to occur in the same proportion in documents. The rows of V^T represent the documents, as projected into a space of rank equal to the number of distinct documents. In this section, we discuss the interpretation of the columns of U and the rows of V^T.

4.1   Term Vectors

By construction, the columns of U are arranged so that the most important vectors are to the left of less important vectors. It can be shown that the entries in the first (leftmost) column of U are non-negative. In other words, the first column indicates which terms tend to occur in all documents, and in what proportion. The first column is not the corpus centroid, but it can be thought of as a weighted intersection. Entries in the other columns may be positive or negative; a negative entry for one term implies that when some other terms are present in a document, the term with the negative entry is less likely to be present.

Recall that each column of U represents a linear combinations of terms that tend to occur together in a consistent fashion throughout the corpus, in the sense that when one of the terms occur, the others do also, and in a certain (but probabilistic) proportion. The vast majority of entries in any one column are close to zero, since most of the terms aren't involved in that particular combination. Except in the first column, some entries are negative, indicating that when some other terms do appear in a document, the negative terms do not.

Interpretation of the columns of U is therefore a matter of seeing which terms have relatively large positive or negative entries. One approach is to simply list the terms for which the corresponding entries are some number of standard deviations away (positive or negative) from the average. Terms that have such large values tend to characterize the column in question.

In a mono-lingual corpus, such as the AP test corpus, the terms in the first column will be those words that occur most often, in most documents, in the same proportion. This may include stopwords, but it may also include markup or domain-specific terms that just happen to occur in most or all documents.

4.2   Document Vectors

The rows of V^T, also known as the "right" singular vectors, represent the documents in the corpus projected into the space $R^{rank(A)}$. The SVD calculation does not change the order of the documents, so row i of V^T corresponds to column (document) i of the original term-document matrix. It can be shown that the entries in row i of the matrix $\Sigma \times V^T$ are document i's coordinates in the new space. The basis for this space is the set of term vectors, in the sense that each column of U is an axis in the new space. (Recall that the columns of U are orthonormal.) So each document has coordinates along the axes defined by each of the columns of U. If two documents (i.e. two rows of the matrix ΣV^T) have a high value for a given coordinate i, it could be said that those two documents are strong in whatever characteristic is represented by column U_i.

In the graphs in Figure 3, the values for each of the 15 coordinates, namely the columns of the matrix ΣV^T, are plotted as a function of document number. Note that all documents have a positive value for the first coordinate.

Let's consider the second coordinate in greater detail. Documents 76 and 139 have the two highest values, while documents 30, 101 and 213 have the lowest values. (Documents 1-73 date from January 1 of 1989, and documents 74-225 date from January 2.) We might therefore expect documents 76 and 139 to be similar in some respect, and documents 30, 101 and 213 to be similar in the opposite respect, whatever that is. The headlines from those documents are shown below.

30	New Year: Promises Of Peace, Bursts Of Violence
76	Operation Rescue Head: Create 'Social Tension' To Change Laws
101	Earthquake, Boat Disaster Rock New Year
139	Operation Rescue Head: Create 'Social Tension' To Change Laws
213	Long-Term AIDS Survivors Defy Odds

The two documents 76 and 139 are so very similar because 139 is a later version of 76, with two minor corrections. Documents 30 and 101 have an obvious common theme, namely some sort of disaster in the midst of New Year celebrations. Document 213 is a set of shorter stories, related to progress in various fields of medical research, including AIDS and artificial organs. The scores for documents 30, 101 and 213 are in fact very close, indicating that they're not very different along this dimension.

5   Related Work

The use of the SVD in text retrieval is discussed in Deerwester *et al* [4]. The effectiveness of SVD as compared to other techniques is addressed in (among other places) the TREC-4 overview [6]. The computational aspects of SVD are discussed in detail in Berry [1]. Our discussion of the dyadic decomposition is based on Berry and Dumais [2]. The use of SVD in multilingual queries, to which we alluded in Section 3, is discussed in detail in the Landauer *et al* patent [8].

The question of writing style was studied by Kjell and Frieder [7], using the Karhunen-Loève Transform, or KLT . The KLT allows the corpus to be mapped into a smaller-dimension space. Kjell and Frieder, for example, studied

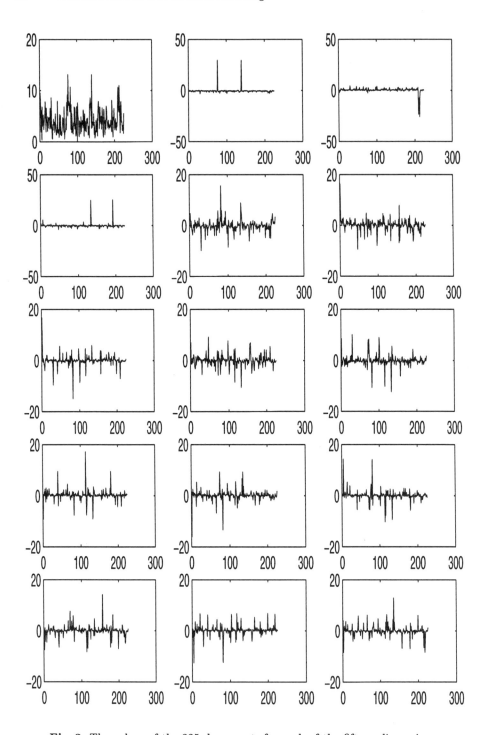

Fig. 3. The values of the 225 documents for each of the fifteen dimensions.

the authorship of the Federalist Papers by mapping those documents into the Cartesian plane. They found that the eleven documents of disputed authorship were mapped into the same region as those documents known to be written by James Madison, indicating that he was also the author of the papers of disputed authorship.

6   Conclusion

We have addressed the question of how to use the SVD to detect topics in a large, dynamic, heterogeneous collection of documents. Previous work on the SVD has tended to focus on its application in text retrieval, as opposed to topical analysis on a collection-wide level. Our contribution is a set of techniques for interpreting of the "term" and "document" vectors generated by the SVD calculation. We can identify the specific combinations of n-grams that are prominent in the term vectors, and evaluate them to see if they represent new or existing topics. The document vectors can be used to spot sets of documents that have unusually high or low values in a particular dimension, indicating that those documents may deal with the same topic.

References

1. Michael Berry. Large scale singular value calculations. *International Journal of Supercomputer Applications*, 6:13–49, 1992.
2. Michael Berry, Susan Dumais, and Gavin O'Brien. Using linear algebra for intelligent information retrieval. *SIAM Review*, 37(4):573–595, December 1995.
3. M. Damashek. Gauging similarity with n-grams: Language-independent categorization of text. *Science*, 267:843–848, 10 February 1995.
4. Scott Deerwester, Susan T. Dumais, George W. Furnas, Thomas K. Landauer, and Richard Harshman. Indexing by latent semantic analysis. *Journal of the American Society for Information Science*, 41:391–407, 1990.
5. Susan Dumais. Improving the retrieval of information from external sources. *Behavior Research Methods, Instruments & Computers*, 23(2):229–236, 1991.
6. Donna Harman. Overview of the Fourth Text REtrieval Conference (TREC-4). National Institute of Standards and Technology, 1995.
7. Bradley Kjell and Ophir Frieder. Visualization of literary style. In *IEEE International Conference on Systems, Man and Cybernetics*, pages 656–661. IEEE, 18-21 October 1992.
8. Thomas Landauer and Michael Littman. Computerized cross-language document retrieval using latent semantic indexing. United States Patent 5,301,109, 5 April 1994.

A Linear Algebra Approach to Language Identification

Laura A. Mather

Computer Science Department, University of Colorado
mather@cs.colorado.edu

Abstract. Identification of the language of documents has tradition-
ally been accomplished using dictionaries or other such language sources.
This paper presents a novel algorithm for identifying the language of documents using much less information about the language than traditional
methods. In addition, if no information about the language of incoming
documents is known, the algorithm groups the documents into language
groups, despite the deficit of language knowledge. The algorithm is based
on the vector space model of information retrieval and uses a matrix projection operator and the singular value decomposition to identify terms
that distinguish between languages. Experimental results show that the
algorithm works reasonably well.

1 Introduction and Motivation

Because of the growth in the amount of electronic information accessible to
various text applications it is now necessary to classify text documents by language. Although some HTML formats allow language tagging, many applications
still do not have a facility for identifying the language of the document. Since
documents are usually not tagged with their corresponding language, it is the
responsibility of the application (whether it is a retrieval application or some
other application) to determine the language of a document.

Some researchers would suggest that the problem of language identification
(classifying documents by language) has been solved. Given a set of electronic
dictionaries in the languages that documents could appear in, it is simple to score
the words in a document by the dictionaries in which they appear and therefore
determine the language of a document. There is one main problem with this
approach: at this time, not only are there very few electronic dictionaries, but
also their coverage, the number of words from the language that they contain,
is often limited. In addition, in order to use this approach for the language
identification problem, it is necessary to know the set of possible languages before
processing the documents. In some situations this is difficult or impossible.

Damashek [1] presents another method for classifying documents by language
where documents are represented as vectors of n-gram counts. The n-gram counts
are found by sliding an n-character window along the text of a document and
counting each occurrence of the sequence of characters in the window. To determine similarity of documents, the document vectors are compared using a cosine

measure (the cosine of the angle between two documents). Documents written in the same language were shown to have high similarity scores in this context.

Grefenstette [5] summarizes two other methods that identify the language of electronic texts. One approach tokenizes example texts (one million characters per languages) into trigrams (sequences of three letter occurrences) and assigns each trigram a probability of occurring in each language. To classify a document of unknown language, the probability of the sequence of trigrams in that document is calculated for each language and the language with the highest probability is returned as the language of the document.

Grefenstette's second technique uses words with five characters or less. The training set of one million characters per language is tokenized into words. The number of occurrences for each of the small words (five characters or less) is counted for each language and those that occur more than three times are retained. The frequencies of these words are then transformed into probabilities, as in the trigram case. An incoming text is tokenized into small words, and the probability of the document being classified as a particular language is the product of the probabilities of the words for each language. Again, the language with the highest probability is returned as the language of the document.

The language identification method in this paper uses the vector space model as it is applied to information retrieval. Documents are represented as m-dimensional vectors, where m is the total number of terms that occur in the document set. A term-document matrix for a document set with n documents is an $m \times n$ matrix where the rows correspond to the terms in the document set and the columns correspond to the documents. In the simplest sense, an element in a term-document matrix A is a_{ij}, where a_{ij} is the number of times that term i occurs in document j. There are various weighting schemes that scale the values a_{ij} based on various properties of the term-document matrix A, but for the purposes of this paper, the raw term counts are sufficient.

This paper introduces an algorithm for classifying electronic documents by language. The algorithm identifies the terms in a term-document matrix that are highly correlated. The distribution of the highly correlated terms across the documents defines a group of documents. This grouping is then used to separate documents into classes corresponding to language. This algorithm groups documents by language using a very small amount of information about the document languages, certainly less information than the standard, electronic dictionary, method. The highly correlated terms are found using a matrix projection and singular value decomposition of the term-document matrix.

The next section outlines the projection operator and the singular value decomposition of matrices. Then the algorithm for classifying documents by languages is described and the experimental results of the algorithm are presented. Finally, the last section gives some conclusions as well as the future work to be done on the algorithm.

2   Linear Algebra Background

This section discusses two linear algebra ideas: a matrix projection operator and
the singular value decomposition of a matrix. The projection operator and the
singular value decomposition are referred to later in this paper. The language
identification algorithm presented in the next section uses the matrix projection
operator and the singular value decomposition of a term-document matrix to
identify the terms that discriminate between documents in the document set.
These terms are then used to group the documents in the document set by
language.

2.1   The Matrix Projection Operator

The matrix projection operator described in this section is based on a clustering
algorithm by Marron and McCloskey [6]. In this algorithm, the rows and columns
of a rectangular matrix (the term-document matrix in our case) are normalized
so that they are orthogonal to the all ones vector. Marron and McCloskey apply
the projection described in this section to both the rows and the columns. Since
the language identification algorithm is only concerned with the terms of the
matrix (and therefore, the rows), this projection operator is only applied to the
rows.

Given a term-document matrix $A \in \Re^{m \times n}$, define a centering matrix C_m by

$$C_m = I_m - \frac{1}{m} 1_m 1_m^T , \qquad (1)$$

where I_m is the $m \times m$ identity matrix and 1_m is the m long vector of all ones.
The row centered matrix A' is then defined as

$$A' = C_m * A . \qquad (2)$$

Since C_m is merely a projection onto the orthogonal complement of the span
of 1_m, 2 has the effect of centering all of the columns of A. In other words, the
sum of each column of A' is exactly 0.0. Statistically, this can be interpreted as
subtracting the mean of the column from every element in the column (therefore,
giving the columns of A' mean 0.0). The matrix projection operator will be used
with the singular value decomposition to identify highly correlated terms.

2.2   The Singular Value Decomposition

The singular value decomposition (SVD) of matrices is used in several applications to information retrieval [2, 3] as well as in many other areas. In this section
the SVD and some of its properties are defined. The SVD can be used to produce
low-order approximations to the original term-document matrix. One of these
low-order approximations is used, with the matrix projection operator, in the
language identification algorithm to separate terms into groups that are highly
correlated.

The SVD of a matrix $A \in \Re^{m \times n}$ is the decomposition of A into three matrices, $U \in \Re^{m \times m}$, $S \in \Re^{m \times n}$ and $V \in \Re^{n \times n}$ such that

$$A = USV^T \ , \tag{3}$$

where U and V are orthogonal and S is diagonal [4].

The columns of U are the left singular vectors of A (and, therefore, the eigenvectors of AA^T). The columns of V are the right singular vectors of A (and the eigenvectors of $A^T A$). The matrix S is a diagonal matrix with the elements, σ_i on the diagonal occurring in decreasing order. These diagonal elements are called the "singular values" of the matrix A and their squares (σ_i^2) are eigenvalues of both AA^T and $A^T A$. It should be noted here that although the singular values are unique, the U and V matrices are not necessarily unique. If any of the singular values of A has multiplicity greater than one there are orthogonal transformations of the U and V matrices that are also valid left and right singular vectors of the matrix A.

Some important properties of a matrix A are determined from its SVD. For example, the rank of A, which we denote r, is equal to the number of nonzero singular values in S. This implies that if a matrix is rank-deficient, it will have some singular values exactly equal to 0.0. Also,

$$null(A) = span\{v_{r+1}, \ldots, v_n\} \ , \tag{4}$$

where $null(A)$ is the null space of A and v_i is the ith column of the matrix V. Finally, the range of A is equal to

$$range(A) = span\{u_1, \ldots, u_r\} \ , \tag{5}$$

where u_i is the ith column of the matrix U.

In addition, the elements of the singular value decomposition of a matrix can be used to obtain a best rank-k approximation to that matrix. For example, the first singular triple of A, (σ_1, u_1, v_1), where σ_1 is the first singular value of A and u_1 and v_1 are the first left and right singular vectors, respectively, can be used to obtain the best rank-1 approximation to A, namely

$$A_1 = \sigma_1 u_1 v_1^T \ . \tag{6}$$

The effect of using the matrix projection operator with the singular value decomposition is now described. Consider the centered matrix A' described in Sect. 2.1. The singular value decomposition of the centered matrix is defined as

$$A' = U'S'V'^T \ , \tag{7}$$

where, again, U' and V' are orthogonal matrices containing the left and right singular values of A', respectively, and S' is a diagonal matrix where the values on the diagonal of S' are the singular values of A'. Since U' and V' are orthogonal transformations of A', they will maintain the row and column structure of A'. Therefore, since the columns of A' have zero mean, the columns of U' are also centered and have zero mean. (If we had also centered the rows, the rows of V' would also be centered.)

In particular, consider the first left singular vector of the matrix A', u'_1. Since u'_1 has zero mean and u'_1 is the first left singular vector of A', the elements in u'_1 can be grouped into two classes: positive elements and nonpositive elements. Because of the structure of u'_1, the rows of A corresponding to the positive elements of u'_1 will be highly correlated with each other. In addition, these rows will be negatively correlated with the rows corresponding to nonpositive values in u'_1. Similarly, the rows of A corresponding to the nonpositive elements of u'_1 are highly correlated with each other and negatively correlated with the rows corresponding to the positive elements of u'_1. This fact will be used in the following section which described the language classification algorithm.

3   Language Classification

Since the language identification problem has been solved in the cases where electronic dictionaries for all languages of interest are available, the algorithm in this paper attempts to identify languages when much less about the possible languages is known. This section defines the algorithm for classifying documents by language. Details about what is required as input to the algorithm are given as well as what can be expected as output. Finally, some experimental results are also given.

3.1   The Algorithm

The theory behind this algorithm for classifying documents by language is an extension of the Marron-McCloskey clustering algorithm [6]. In this paper, the Marron-McCloskey algorithm has been modified to only consider the rows of the matrix (and therefore the terms of the term-document matrix). Also, the algorithm presented here accounts for a fairly large amount of noise that may occur in a term-document matrix. First, an outline of the algorithm is given. Next, some details of the algorithm are explained.

The basic idea of the algorithm is to identify terms that discriminate between languages. Using these discriminating terms, documents are separated into language groups. Terms that are not useful for discriminating between languages are called stopwords and are identified by the algorithm and discarded. The input to the algorithm is a term-document matrix generated from documents from one or more languages. The algorithm returns an approximate grouping of documents from the term-document matrix where the groups correspond to language.

It may not be clear why the algorithm separates documents into language groups instead of some other type of grouping. Highly correlated terms are those that occur together very frequently. When a document set contains documents from more than one language, the frequently occurring terms are used in only a subset of the documents, those documents that correspond to the same language. Therefore, in the case of a multi-lingual document set, the terms are isolated by co-occurrence frequency and the documents are grouped by language. If the document set contains documents from a single language, the correlation of terms would be based on something other than the frequently occurring terms since these would likely be considered stopwords by the algorithm and, therefore, discarded.

It should be noted here that the algorithm uses no information about the number of languages in the original term document matrix, the number of documents per language or the terms that correspond to the rows of the matrix. In addition, the order of both the terms and the documents in the term-document matrix is inconsequential to the outcome of the algorithm.

The algorithm for identifying the language of documents has two parts. Part I of the algorithm is iterative. Until prescribed stopping conditions are met, the algorithm recursively partitions the original term-document matrix. Also, the document groups found in Part I tend to be "noisy" (some of the groups will contain documents from other languages). Part II of the algorithm refines the noisy document groups produced in Part I.

Language Identification Algorithm, Part I

1. Create term-document matrix of term counts, call it A.
2. Normalize A so that all of the rows sum to 1.0.
3. Test whether A contains only stopwords or only discriminating terms.
4. If A contains both stopwords and discriminating terms (condition in Step 3 is not met):
   (a) Find the projection of A, $A' = C_m * A$ as defined in Sect. 2.1.
   (b) Find the SVD of A', $A' = U'S'V'^T$.
   (c) Use the first left singular vector of A' to divide the rows of A into two highly correlated sets. Create new term-document matrices from each of these sets of terms and pass each of these matrices into Step 3 of Part I.
5. If the condition in Step 3 is met, determine whether A contains stopwords or discriminating terms.
6. If A contains stopwords, identify and discard them.
7. If A contains discriminating terms, determine which documents these terms discriminate and save this list of documents as a potential document group.

Language Identification Algorithm, Part II

1. Given all potential document groups identified by Part I, create an $n \times n$ co-occurrence matrix, B, where b_{ij} is the number of times document i occurs in a potential group with document j.
2. Threshold B by setting all b_{ij} which are less than some value (say, *thresh1*) to 0.0.
3. Run Part I of this algorithm on the matrix B. The result of this step is an improved grouping (by language) of the documents from the original matrix A.

It is necessary to normalize the rows of the matrix A in Step 2 of Part I of the algorithm since rows corresponding to terms that occur with high frequency will be grouped together by the algorithm, irregardless of whether they are discriminating terms, stopwords or both.

If the first two singular values of a matrix, say $\tilde{\sigma}_1$ and $\tilde{\sigma}_2$, are similar, and the rows of the matrix have been normalized as in Step 2 of Part I of the algorithm, then it is likely that the matrix contains only discriminating terms or only stopwords. If these two singular values are not similar, then it is likely that the matrix contains both stopwords and discriminating terms. Therefore, the equation

$$\frac{\tilde{\sigma}_1}{\tilde{\sigma}_2} < 1 + \epsilon \ , \tag{8}$$

where ϵ is some small value, can be used to determine whether a matrix contains a combination of stopwords and discriminating terms. If 8 is true, then the matrix in question contains only stopwords or only discriminating terms. If it is false, then the matrix contains both types of terms and should be partitioned again.

If a matrix contains both stopwords and discriminating terms, it is possible to split this matrix into two matrices in an attempt to meet the stopping condition of Step 3 of Part I of the algorithm. Using the singular value decomposition of the matrix projection of A as in the Marron-McCloskey algorithm [6], it is possible to divide the terms of A into two sets, creating two new term-document matrices. Then the stopping condition of Step 3 can be checked for each of these new matrices.

If the matrix A contains only stopwords or only discriminating terms, it is relatively easy to determine which of these two cases is present. Since stopwords occur with either extremely high or extremely low frequency, it is possible to use the number of times a term occurs in the document set to determine whether that term is a stopword or not. If the term occurs with moderate frequency, it is a discriminating term. Otherwise, it is a stopword. The algorithm shown above gives sets of terms that are either all stopwords or all discriminating terms. Therefore, the term count method can be averaged over all terms in a matrix to determine whether the terms in the matrix are discriminating or not.

Sets of terms that are all stopwords can be discarded at this point. Sets of terms that are discriminating terms can be used to group the documents in the document set by language in the following way. Given a term-document matrix that contains only discriminating terms, sum the columns of the matrix. Then the documents corresponding to columns with a sum greater than some threshold (say, $thresh2$) are potentially of the same language. These documents should be grouped together for further processing in Part II of the algorithm.

The document groups found above tend to be noisy. Part II of the algorithm reduces the noise of these groups in order to find a better approximation to the true groups of the documents in A. First, a grouping co-occurrence matrix, B, is created. The elements in the matrix B are thresholded to reduce the noise in B, then Part I of the algorithm is run on B to find the true groups.

It should be noted that the computational expense of this algorithm may be misleading. Since the SVD is an expensive computation, and many SVD's are calculated through the iterations of this algorithm, it may seem that the algorithm is very expensive computationally. In fact, since only the first left singular vector and two singular values are needed, it is possible to reduce the computational expense of the SVD by using a variant of the power method to compute only these values. Since the power method is much less expensive than the SVD, the use of this method decreases the computational cost of the algorithm a great deal. In addition, it should be noted that since the original matrix is partitioned at each iteration, the size of the resulting SVD's is also reduced.

3.2   The Experiments

This section describes the experiments that were performed to test the language identification algorithm presented in Sect. 3.1. First, the experimental design is given. This includes a description of the data set that was used as well as descriptions of the types of experiments that were performed. Next, the results of the experiments are summarized.

Experimental Design   The experiments performed on the language identification algorithm used a subset of the documents in the European Corpus Initiative Multilingual Corpus 1 data set which was produced and distributed by the Association for Computational Linguistics. The original corpus contains documents in 23 languages in addition to documents that contain text in multiple languages. The experimental corpus used for this paper was a subset of the original corpus. Documents from eight of the original 23 languages had to be eliminated for various reasons such as not enough documents in that language (languages with fewer than five documents were not used) or texts for documents not in extended ASCII (which was the only text that the algorithm could process).

The 15 languages in the experimental corpus were: Czech, Danish, Dutch, English, French, German, Greek, Italian, Latin, Malay, Portuguese, Serbian, Spanish, Swedish, and Turkish. Content of the documents varied and included such things as newspaper text, excerpts from novels, poetry, and excerpts from dictionaries. The number of documents corresponding to each language in the experimental corpus varied from five (since only languages with five or more documents were used) to 150. Since the documents varied in length, the first 5k bytes of text were used as the representative of each document. If the original document contained less than 5k bytes of text, then all of the original document was used. Also, values for *thresh*1 and *thresh*2 were selected before the experiments were run and did not change throughout the course of the experiments. Recall that *thresh*1 is the threshold for the elements in the co-occurrence matrix B and *thresh*2 is the threshold that determines which documents, from a term-document matrix of discriminating terms, should be included in a potential language group. If, in practice, any information about the document set is known (for example, the number of documents per language or the number of languages occurring in the document set) the thresholds can be adjusted accordingly.

The experiments performed for this paper were fairly small, with a maximum of 40 documents in the term-document matrix. The purpose of using a small number of documents per experiment was to allow careful analysis of the document sets and a better understanding of the mechanism of the algorithm. In addition, it was hypothesized that the language identification algorithm would perform well with very little knowledge about each language. The small number of documents per language helped to evaluate the validity of this hypothesis. The section on future work includes discussion on larger experiments to be performed.

There were two types of experiments performed. In the first type of experiment four languages were randomly selected from the 15 possible languages. Then, 10 documents were randomly selected from the set of documents from each of these four languages. If the document set from a particular language contained less than 10 documents, all documents from this language were used. A term-document matrix was then created from this set of 40 (or fewer) documents and the algorithm from Sect. 3.1 was applied to this matrix.

In the second type of experiment, languages were selected at random from the set of 15 possible languages. All documents in each subsequent language were added to the experimental set until the set contained 40 documents. There were two constraints on this experiment. First, if the document set for a language had more than 25 documents in it, only 25 (randomly selected) documents were added to the set. Second, if there were more documents in a language document set than were needed to complete the experimental set of 40 documents, then the documents needed to complete the experimental set were selected randomly from the language document set. The results of these experiments are now given.

Experimental Results A total of 100 experiments were performed, 50 of each of the random types described above. There are two possible errors in the experimental groups: misclassification of documents and not classifying documents. Table 1 summarizes the results of the experiments based on these two types of errors. Misclassification occurs when some set of documents from one language is grouped with documents from another language. In the 100 randomized experiments, 3841 documents were classified (note that some documents were used in more than one experiment). Misclassification error occurred in 38 of the 100 random experiments, resulting in the misclassification of 307 of the 3841 documents (approximately 8%).

Spanish was the most commonly misclassified language, producing misclassification error in 17 experiments. Spanish was misclassified with documents in Italian, Portuguese, English and French. English was misclassified with documents from other languages in 15 experiments. In most cases English was misgrouped with documents in French and Spanish.

Additional analysis identifies a possible reason for the misclassification of English documents with French and Spanish documents. The experimental doc-

Table 1. Classification errors from 100 experiments classifying 3841 documents.

Error Type	Exps with that Error	Docs with that Error
misclassified	38	307
not classified	34	129

ument set contains parallel documents from English, Spanish and French: documents that are exact translations of each other. Approximately 20 documents are direct translations of each other in these three languages. Normally, these parallel documents would not have any effect on the performance of the language identification algorithm. The problem with this particular set of parallel documents, though, is their formatting.

In each of these parallel documents, approximately 25% of the words are "tab" characters. Because the "tab" character in this document set is represented by the token "htab", the parser assumed that "htab" was a word in the documents. When the language identification algorithm clustered the documents based on correlation between terms, it found that the correlation of the "htab" tokens was stronger than the correlation of the language terms for these documents. Therefore, documents with many "htab" tokens were grouped together instead of being grouped by language. It is believed that this accounts for at least 20% of the misclassification errors encountered in this study.

Of the experiments with misclassification error, 11 experiments involved misclassification of Turkish. There did not appear to be a pattern as to which languages the Turkish documents were classified with. The other common misclassification errors were: Portuguese, Spanish and Italian were often classified together, and Latin was grouped with both Portuguese and Italian.

It appears that the main reason for misclassification error was experiments that did not contain enough documents from a particular language to isolate discriminating terms from that language. Of the 38 experiments with misclassification errors, 32 of those errors occurred when the number of documents from a language was 10 or less. Experiments with more documents per language (10 to 25 documents) resulted in much more accurate groupings of the documents. In addition, it is possible that some of the noise from Part I of the algorithm caused misclassification error. This could be eliminated by adjusting the thresholds of the algorithm.

The second type of error occurs when documents are not assigned to any group. In 34 of the 100 experiments some set of documents was not assigned to any group. Of the 3841 documents classified in the experiments, 129 of them were not a language class. In particular, the Turkish documents were often not classified, making up 112 of the 129 documents which were not classified. This problem with the Turkish documents, as well as their misclassification errors, gives further indication of an anomaly in the Turkish documents that needs to be investigated further.

Not assigning documents to any language group could happen for one of two reasons: the classification algorithm found that all of the terms in the document were stopwords or Part II of the algorithm could not discriminate between some set of documents and the noise from the other documents. The latter of these two cases is caused by a low value of *thresh*1 from Part II of the algorithm and initial examination found this to be the cause for non classification a majority of the time. Since only 17 of the documents, other than the Turkish documents, were not assigned to groups, this indicates that the threshold that was used for the noise in Part II of the algorithm was fairly good.

4   Discussion and Future Work

This paper presents on algorithm for classifying documents by language. The algorithm uses a matrix projection operator and the singular value decomposition to find terms that discriminate between languages. It then uses these discriminating terms to group the documents by language. Since the algorithm operates solely on the term-document matrix, it is not restricted by the text format of the document set. The algorithm is only limited by the document parser since it is the parser that creates the term-document matrix. Therefore, the algorithm is applicable to all text formats that can be parsed electronically.

Initial experiments show that the algorithm is susceptible to two types of errors: misclassification of documents and non classification of documents. When the number of documents per language in the document set is small, these documents often get misclassified. More work needs to be done to determine the number of documents necessary to accurately classify the documents in a document set. It is anticipated that 10 to 20 documents will be sufficient to maintain high classification accuracy, but this needs to be verified. In addition, it is possible that adjusting the value of *thresh*1 will reduce the noise in the B matrix and eliminate some of the misclassification.

The case where documents are not assigned to any group does not appear to be a problem. Since this occurred very few times (other than with one anomalous language), it is likely that this would not be a problem in practice. Some changes in the values of *thresh*1 or *thresh*2 could reduce the number of documents that are not classified (though adjusting *thresh*1 in this way may have an adverse effect on misclassification). Some work needs to be done to understand why the set of Turkish documents behaved so strangely in comparison to the other documents in the set.

In five of the 100 random experiments, documents from one language were put into more than one group. It is believed that these groups separate documents by some other characteristic than language (possibly by topic characteristics or by the genre of the document). Additional work needs to be done to determine the reason that documents from the same language are sometimes classified into different groups. The algorithm presented in this paper still needs to be compared with other language classification (both dictionary and non-dictionary) algorithms. This could be done by running several algorithms on the same experiments and comparing their performances.

In conclusion, it appears that the algorithm presented in this paper is useful for grouping documents by language. The technique presented here is unique in its use of linear algebra to classify documents. Also, it uses much less information than traditional dictionary methods. Initial experiments show that the algorithm performs reasonably well on the test data. Future work needs to be done to test the algorithm on larger data sets. In addition some variations of the thresholds of the algorithm need to be explored.

Acknowledgements. The author would like to thank Joe McCloskey for his insightful comments. In addition, thanks go to Kristin Jackson and Chris Marron for their technical assistance.

References

1. Marc Damashek. Gauging similarity with n-grams: Language-independent categorization of text. *Science*, 267:843–848, 1995.
2. Scott Deerwester, Susan T. Dumais, George W. Furnas, Thomas K. Landauer, and Richard Harshman. Indexing by latent semantic analysis. *Journal of the American Society for Information Science*, 41(6):391–407, 1990.
3. Susan T. Dumais. Improving the retrieval of information from external sources. *Behavior Research Methods, Instruments & Computers*, 23(2):229–236, 1991.
4. Gene H. Golub and Charles F. Van Loan. *Matrix Computations*. The Johns Hopkins University Press, Baltimore, 1989.
5. Gregory Grefenstette. Comparing two language identification schemes. In *Proceedings of the 3rd International Conference on Statistical Analysis of Textual Data*, 1995.
6. Chris Marron and Joe McCloskey. Optimal partitions and clustering. In *Proceedings of the 1997 Conference on Linear Algebra and Applications*. SIAM, 1997.

Indexed Tree Matching with Complete Answer Representations

Holger Meuss

Center for Information and Language Processing, University of Munich
meuss@cis.uni-muenchen.de,
WWW home page: http://www.cis.uni-muenchen.de/people/meuss

Abstract. This paper picks up the Tree Matching approach to integrate the paradigm of structured documents into the field of Information Retrieval. The concept of Tree Matching is extended by the notion of complete answer representations (CARs), which makes it possible to avoid the combinatorial explosion in the number of solutions (and thus complexity). An algorithm is presented that combines a class of Tree Matching problems with index-based search and returns a CAR in linear time.

1 Introduction

During the last years, considerable effort has been put into the integration of structured documents into the field of Information Retrieval. Various systems have been proposed, providing facilities to query a set of documents on structure and content level (see [NBY96] and [Loe94] for surveys). These queries provide the user with a powerful instrument: She may query for instance for all letters containing a subject line somehow related to the term "insurance". She can select out of a document pool all articles that are referred to from a given set of articles. If a system also provides facilities to manipulate text, the user can create different versions of books, compose product catalogues out of existing documents or update these catalogues with queries like "Double the price of all cars older than 15 years and add the word 'Oldtimer' to the description".

The common view on structured documents distinguishes between the structure of a document and its actual content (flat text). If structure is represented explicitly, a document is seen as a directed graph of nodes, with the nodes corresponding to structural elements of the document, e.g. chapters or headings. By requiring additional properties of this graph, e.g. tree structure, the various models define the class of documents they are able to represent. These models have subsequently different query facilities.

This work picks up a formalism proposed in [Kil92] and [KM93]: Tree Matching is a formal model for querying a structured document database. It provides the user with a highly expressive and data independent query language. The major drawback of this formalism is its bad time complexity, which is polynomial[1]. This complexity is model inherent, since the model is able to express tuple-like answers (namely variable substitutions), and therefore prone to combinatorial explosion. Other models (like Proximal Nodes: [NBY95]) avoid this problem by restricting the expressiveness of the query language. Additionally, Tree Matching made no explicit statement on how to integrate indices into the query evaluation. But indices are essential for any practical application of Tree Matching.

Here, we take Tree Matching as a starting point, but we propose a compact representation of solutions called complete answer representation (CAR) that avoids a brute enumeration of all solutions. It is shown that in this way the evaluation of Tree Matching becomes linear. In addition the paper proposes an integration of indices into the evaluation of Tree Matching. The index accesses are expressed by constraint expressions, which provide a substantial and flexible extension of the Tree Matching formalism.

By integrating the concept of an index into the formalism, and by introducing a compact representation of solutions, this paper revives the original ideas proposed in [Kil92] and [KM93], and shifts them further from pure algebraic model to software reality.

2   Tree Matching

In this section we review Tree Matching as introduced in [Kil92] and [KM93]. The structure of documents is captured by the concept of labeled and ordered trees: The documents are hierarchically organized into labeled elements that contain other elements. The leaves of the trees are filled with portions of the flat text (Figure 1).

In a query the user selects documents on the basis of their structure and content, e.g. "Give me all documents that have a subsection whose title contains the words 'Tree Matching'." The query is represented as a tree (pattern tree), and query evaluation means to search for a mapping that maps the pattern tree to the target tree (document database). This mapping has to respect various relations between the nodes in the two trees, e.g. ancestorship or order.

By distinguishing the different relations, [Kil92] defines ten different Tree Matching problems, of which the most interesting for document databases are ordered and unordered tree inclusion. A pattern tree is *included in* the target tree, if there is a mapping f that maps every node v of the pattern tree to a node $f(v)$ of the target tree, so that all ancestors of v are mapped to ancestors of $f(v)$ in the target tree. If in addition the horizontal order relation between the nodes of the pattern tree is preserved, the pattern tree is *included with order in* the target tree.

In addition, the leaves of the pattern tree can be replaced by logical variables and other nodes may be attached with logical variables, in order to specify equalities between different parts of the pattern tree. The effect of this construction

---

[1] Only data complexity is considered in this paper, i.e. the complexity is related to the size of the database, whereas the size of queries is considered to be fixed.

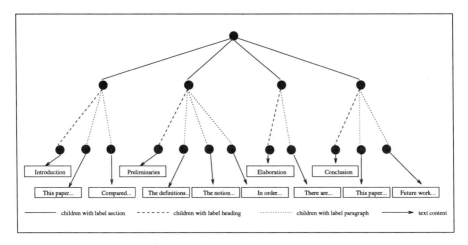

Fig. 1. A part of a document database

is similar to the join in relational databases and allows queries like "Give me all articles that are referenced from this article."

A query can even consist of a set of pattern trees, being connected via variables. These pattern trees are evaluated simultaneously.

Algorithms and Complexity In [Kil92] various algorithms are introduced that solve the different classes of Tree Matching problems. For the most general case, unordered tree inclusion, these algorithms have polynomial time complexity. But if the query contains no variables and the document database is restricted to nonperiodic trees, i.e. trees that do not contain the same label twice in a path, a linear time algorithm for finding one solution is presented. This algorithm compares the target in a top-down fashion with the query. Unfortunately an algorithm providing *all* solutions cannot be linear, since the number of solutions for a query is polynomial in the size of the database. This holds for most of the proposed Tree Matching problems, including tree inclusion and path inclusion.

3   Tree Matching Revisited

This section describes the integration of indices and complete answer representations into the Tree Matching formalism.

3.1   Syntax

This paper uses a representation for queries in the form of linear tree descriptions with constraints. This differs slightly from the formalism presented in [KM93], in being more explicit about relations between the nodes. Of course, this representation is not intended to be used by the end user.

Structural and flat aspects of the text are separated more rigidly than in [Kil92]:

The query is composed of a structural part and a constraint part that describes mainly flat aspects of the text[2].

A *query* is a conjunction of linear tree descriptions followed by a constraint expression. A *linear tree description (LTD)* is a term, whose function symbols (labels) are strings, "*", "+" or ".". To each subterm we may attach a variable (denoted by a capital letter). The arguments of a subterm are separated by either "," (for ordered Tree Matching) or ";" (for unordered Tree Matching). A mixture between ordered and unordered arguments (e.g. section(title;par,par) is not possible for siblings, and the variables occuring in a LTD have to be distinct.

A *constraint expression* is introduced by the keyword "with", followed by a conjunction of constraints. In this work, only one constraint type is proposed, although there is a broad range of constraints that can be treated efficiently. The constraint is X including string, where X is a variable, and string is an arbitrary string.

In the following, LTDs are identified with the tree described by the term. Nodes with function symbol *, + or . are called *don't care nodes*, the others *label nodes*. To keep the presentation clear, it is assumed that the queries consist of exactly one LTD and a conjunction of constraints.

Example 5. The following query selects books out of a document database that include a section whose heading includes the words "document" and "database", and that contains a paragraph including the word "algebra".

```
book(S=section(H=heading;P=paragraph))
with H including "document database" and
P including "algebra"
```

3.2   Semantics

The *meaning of a query* in a given document database represented as a forest is the answer to the query, which is defined as a set of substitutions for the variables. In the following definition, m denotes a function on query nodes mapping (for a given query) a query node to its parent.

Definition 1. *A function f mapping the nodes of the LTD of a query to the nodes of the document database is called a* query embedding[3] *if the following 5 restrictions are met:*

1. *The root of the LTD is mapped to a root in the target, except if the root of the LTD is a don't care node. Then "*" is mapped to any node in the target, "+" to any node but a root, and "." to any root.*
2. *For every label node v of the query, v and $f(v)$ are required to have the same label.*

---

[2] This notation makes it easy to integrate new types of constraints into the model. Equality constraints are part of this work but not included due to space limitations.

[3] This definition differs from the original Tree Matching formalism, where a query embedding has to be injective in addition.

3. *A query label node v must be mapped to a child of $f(m(v))$. A query node v labeled with "$*$" can be mapped to $f(m(v))$ or any descendant of $f(m(v))$. A query node v labeled with "$+$" can be mapped to any descendant of $f(m(v))$. A query node v labeled with "." can be mapped to any child of $f(m(v))$.*
4. *If v_1 and v_2 are siblings in the query tree divided by "," with v_1 preceding v_2, then $f(v_1)$ must precede $f(v_2)$ in the target.*
5. *If query nodes are constrained via attached variables and constraints, then the respective target nodes must satisfy the constraints: Let u_1 be a query node with attached variable* X. *Then* X *including* text *means that the region associated with $f(u_1)$ includes* text.

A *solution* to a query is a substitution consisting of bindings $X \mapsto f(v)$ for every variable X attached to a node v in the query, where f is a query embedding. An *answer* is the set of all solutions.

Due to the tuple character of solutions, the number of solutions is prone to combinatorial explosion. To avoid this, we introduce the notion of a complete answer representation (CAR):

Definition 2. *A framework (Figure 2) is a labelled tree whose nodes are called slots. Each slot is filled with a sequence of nodes (target candidates) of the target tree. Each target candidate in a slot S is equipped with an array. For each child S' of S this array has exactly one field that contains a list of pointers to target candidates in S'.*
The pointers in the arrays define a directed graph on the set of target candidates in the framework. A framework is connected *if this directed graph is connected. The directed graph is a forest, hence tree-related terminology is applied.*
An instantiation of a framework f *is a connected framework, that has the same slots as f, but contains in every slot only one of the target candidates in the corresponding slot in f.*
A constrained framework *is a framework that has order constraints between the slots. An* instantiation of a constrained framework *is* constraint-respecting *if the target candidates respect the constraints of the respective slots.*
A framework for a query q *is a framework whose slots, edges and labels correspond exactly to the nodes, edges and labels in the query q. If query nodes are associated with a variable, the corresponding slots are associated with the same variable. If the children of a query node are ordered, the corresponding slot is marked with an order constraint.*

An instantiation of a query framework defines in a natural way a mapping from the query nodes to the nodes of the document database, and a substitution for the variables in the query, by mapping every variable to the target candidate contained in the slot associated with that variable.

Definition 3. *A constrained framework for a query q is called* complete answer representation (CAR) *for q and a target, if for every constraint-respecting instantiation the induced substitution is a solution for q and the target, and if for every solution there is a constraint-respecting instantiation of the framework inducing it.*

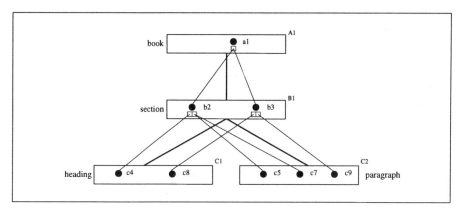

Fig. 2. A connected framework

In order to distinguish the different tree structures, where nodes appear, prefixes are used: First there is the document database (denoted with the prefix "target"), then there is the query ("query"), the slots of a framework ("framework") and the target candidates in a framework ("array") (where the tree structure is defined by the arrays of the target candidates).

Example 6. The framework in Figure 2 consists of the slots $A1, B1, C1$ and $C2$. $B1$ is a framework child of $A1$. The target candidates $c4, c5$ and $c7$ are array children of $b2$. The framework is a query framework for the query in Example 5.

Due to space limitations, the treatment of don't care nodes in queries is not covered in the rest of this paper. They can be integrated into the proposed framework smoothly without major changes.

3.3   Data Model and Storage

The original work on Tree Matching and document databases makes no explicit statement about how to organize the data physically and logically. This paper proposes a storage model that distinguishes three different layers: The content (i.e. flat text), the structure and the index.

The pure content of the documents is stored in the form of flat text without tags in a group of files. The logical structure of each document is represented by a tree, all documents together form a forest. The leaves of the trees have pointers to regions in the flat files associating the leaf with a content region. Every document is associated with the root of its structural tree. Every node has a unique identifier.

An index structure (e.g. a Trie) maps terms (e.g. words) to occurrences in documents. Since documents are trees, the index maps terms to structural components, namely leaves, and the offset of the occurrence relative to the leaf region. For efficiency reasons, the term is mapped to a set of paths, ending in the respective leaves. The way the index is organized and how the terms are derived from the documents (stopword lists, stemming, etc.) is independent from the proposed model and left aside in the following considerations.

3.4   Indexed Tree Matching

Note that the algorithm described in this section is formulated for queries without don't care symbols.[4]

Based on the query, a framework is built and in the course of the algorithm filled with target candidates (together with information about descendant-relations). The general approach to the query evaluation is a mixed bottom-up/top-down approach: Each path of the LTD is evaluated independently from the surrounding query tree in a bottom-up fashion. Then the paths are combined in the query framework in a top-down manner according to the pattern described by the query. The resulting framework together with the order constraints represents a CAR for the query.

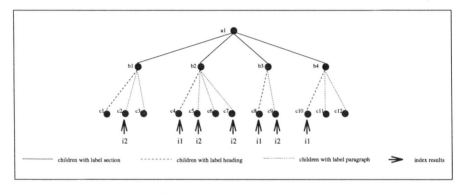

Fig. 3. A document database

In parallel to the description of the algorithm the evaluation of the query introduced in Example 5 is presented. The document database is given by the tree depicted in Figure 3. The example query has two including-constraints that are evaluated with two index accesses i1 and i2. The resulting leaves (and paths) of these accesses are also depicted in Figure 3.

A path p_t in the target is said to *correspond* to a path p_q in a query if the i-th node in p_t and p_q have the same labels for all nodes in p_q. The i-th nodes in p_t and p_q are then said to correspond. In the following description, we do not explicitly distinguish between query nodes and their respective slots in the framework.

---

[4] In the terminology of Tree Matching it is an algorithm for finding all solutions for the ordered or unordered path inclusion problem.

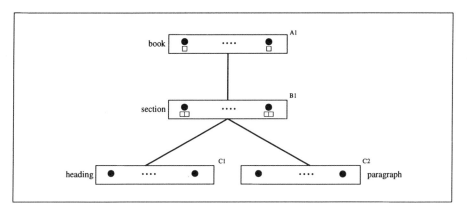

Fig. 4. The framework's initial state

Algorithm for Indexed Tree Matching Given a query and a target database, the following algorithm computes a CAR for the query and target.

A) Construct the initial framework Δ_0 for the query.
B) Evaluate the including-constraints to get the path sets U^i.
C) For every i $(1 \leq i \leq p)$, insert U^i in the framework:
    i.a) Match paths in U^i against Δ_{i-1}, returning $\bar{U}^i$.
    i.b) Match Δ_{i-1} against paths in $\bar{U}^i$, resulting in Δ_i'.
    i.c) Clean the framework Δ_i', resulting in Δ_i.
Result is Δ_p.

Step A):
Construct and return the initial framework Δ_0 for the query, i.e. a framework for the query, where all slots are filled with symbols representing the set of all nodes in the document database, and where the arrays of every node are empty. *The inital query framework for the example query is depicted in Figure 4.*
Step B):
The query is decomposed into paths in the following way: The query has p_1 nodes that are constrained with including constraints, and p_2 unconstrained leaves. Let $p = p_1 + p_2$. Then p_1 index accesses are evaluated, with the i-th access resulting in a set $U^i = \{p_1^i, \ldots, p_{l_i}^i\}$ of paths[5] in the database, each path p_j^i pointing to a leaf containing the respective term. To each unconstrained leaf of the query we assign the set U of all paths in the target. Hence, for $p_1 < j \leq p$ we define $U^j = U$ and $l_j = |U|$ (cardinality of U). Return all U^i.
In addition we define, corresponding to the decomposition of the query, for $1 \leq i \leq p$ the notion of the i-th (partial) framework path in a query framework Θ. *The example query Q has two* including-constraints *that result in two index accesses $i1$ and $i2$. The resulting leaves (and thus paths) of these accesses are depicted in Figure 3. The framework is decomposed into two paths, corresponding to U^1 and U^2: $[A1, B1, C1]$ and $[A1, B1, C2]$.*

---

[5] Paths are required to be full paths, i.e. beginning in a root and ending in a leaf.

Step C.i.a):
Every path in U^i is compared to the i-th framework path in $\varDelta_{i-1}$. Return $\bar{U}_i$, that derives from U_i by discarding all paths not corresponding to the i-th path or including nodes not occurring in the corresponding slots of $\varDelta_{i-1}$.

Step C.i.b):
$\varDelta'_i$ derives from $\varDelta_{i-1}$ in the following way: The slots in the i-th framework path of $\varDelta_{i-1}$ are examined in top-down fashion. Every target candidate in a slot of the examined path in $\varDelta_{i-1}$ not appearing in a path in $\bar{U}^i$ is removed from the slot. For the remaining target candidates, a pointer to the child is entered in the respective field of the array: Let v be a target candidate in a slot that also appears in a path $[v_1, \ldots, v_j, v, v', v_{j+3}, \ldots, v_l]$ in $\bar{U}^i$. Then a pointer to the location of v' in the framework is added in the respective field of the array of v. Note that for $i = 1$, in steps C.1.a) and C.1.b) not all nodes of the target have to be scanned in the slots, since the intersection is trivial in this case: The nodes in the paths U^1 are simply entered in the respective slots and arrays.

Step C.i.c):
For all target candidates u removed in the last step, a cleaning algorithm is triggered: Remove all array descendants of u. Then delete all array ancestors (with all their array descendants) of u having had u as only array descendant in this slot.

In the example there are two sets of paths generated by the index accesses. U^1 has 3 and U^2 has 4 elements. The paths in U^1 are $[a1, b2, c4], [a1, b3, c8]$ and $[a1, b4, c10]$. The first step (C.1) is always trivial, because the slots of the framework are filled with the sets of all nodes initially. Figure 5 depicts the state of the framework after C.1.c).

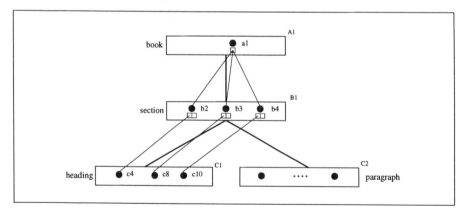

Fig. 5. The framework after inserting U^1

When treating the nodes of U^2 the situation becomes more complicated, since intersection is not trivial. U^2 consists of the paths $[a1, b1, c2], [a1, b2, c5], [a1, b2, c7]$ and $[a1, b3, c9]$. The framework path corresponding to U^2 is $[A1, B1, C2]$. The *first path* $[a1, b1, c2]$ *is removed in step C.2.a), since* $b1$ *does not occur in* $B1$. *The three other paths are entered in step C.2.b), i.e. the pointers are added to the respective fields in the arrays. Note that target candidate* $b4$ *was removed from slot* $B1$, *since it did not occur in a path in* $\bar{U}^2$. *In step C.2.c) the target candidate* $c10$ *was also removed. The result of this step is depicted in Figure 2. Therefore the framework in Figure 2 is the CAR for the query and target.*

Theorem 1. *The framework produced by the algorithm is a CAR for the query.*

Proof. (Sketch) We need to show two assertions:
(1) If Δ is a constraint-respecting instantiation of the framework, then Δ induces a substitution that is a solution for the query and target. We show this by proving that the mapping induced by Δ fulfills the five requirements for a query embedding (Definition 1): The filtering (step C) in the algorithm guarantees 1), 2) and 3). 4) holds since the framework is constraint-respecting. 5 follows from the definition of the U^i (step B).
(2) If there is a solution, there is a constraint-respecting instantiation of the framework inducing the solution. We prove this by showing, that for every query embedding f there is a constraint-respecting instantiation of the framework inducing the embedding: The query embedding f can be identified with a constrained and connected query framework Δ, where every slot is filled with exactly one target candidate. Δ is an instantiation of the framework Θ produced by the algorithm: Every array path in Δ occurs in the corresponding U^i. Therefore these nodes are not deleted in the course of the algorithm and the path information is added gradually in the framework. As a result Δ must be an instantiation of Θ. Δ is obviously constraint-respecting, since f is a query embedding. $\square$

Given a CAR, the (extensional) solutions can be generated with the following simple algorithm (called with the top slot as actual parameter). The algorithm generates all constraint-respecting instantiations of the constrained framework by traversing it in a Prolog-like manner, i.e. using chronological backtracking. The decision marked with (*) is non-deterministic and therefore the backtracking point. The order constraints mentioned in the algorithm derive from ordered arguments (separated by " ,") in the query.

```
Generate solution for actual slot:

Take the next target candidate of the actual slot as
        actual node. (*)
Unify actual node with the variable associated with actual slot.
Generate solution for every field in the array of actual node.
Test if these solutions respect order constraints (if any).
The solution for actual node is composed of
        the solution for the fields (if any) and the actual node.
```

3.5 Complexity

When speaking about complexity in this section, we will always refer to time complexity. Remember that the following complexity results hold for queries without don't care symbols only. We define the size q of a query as the sum of the number of nodes in the LTD and the number of letters in the longest string of the including-constraints in the query, and $l_{max} = max(l_1, \ldots, l_p)$ as the maximal cardinality of the paths sets returned by the index accesses in the query. Note that in the following $l_{max} = n$ (where n is the size of the target) if there is at least one unconstrained leaf.

The complexity of retrieving a CAR is $\mathcal{O}(q^3 * l_{max})$, i.e. a linear data complexity. This can be seen as follows:

The construction of the initial query framework (step A) takes $\mathcal{O}(q)$ steps. Retrieving U^i (step B) takes (when using a Trie) $\mathcal{O}(q)$ computation steps for every i. For all i this step sums up to a complexity $\mathcal{O}(q^2)$.

Entering the nodes into the framework (step C) takes $\mathcal{O}(q^3 * l_{max})$ steps:

For every $1 \le i \le p$ the set U^i as result of the index (or the whole set of paths in the target, for $i > p_1$) is ordered. (The underlying order is the order induced by the target.) The target candidates in the slots are ordered in the same way. There are maximally l_{max} target candidates in the slot and maximally l_{max} paths in U^i (except for $i = 1$). Therefore the intersection between target candidates and and all corresponding nodes in U^i can be computed in $\mathcal{O}(q * l_{max})$ time for all paths at once. (For $i = 1$ the intersection is trivial, since the slots are filled with the set of all nodes in the beginning.) This means that steps C.i.a) and C.i.b) can be computed in $\mathcal{O}(q * l_{max})$.

The cleaning (step C.i.c) for all target candidates removed in the step C.i.b) is of complexity $\mathcal{O}(p * q * l_{max})$, since there are (for $i > 1$) maximally $p * q * l_{max}$ target candidates in the framework, and every target candidate in the framework is visited at most once in the cleaning procedure. (For $i = 1$ no cleaning is necessary, since the nodes are unconnected in the initial state of the framework.) Therefore the complexity of step C.i is $\mathcal{O}(q^2 * l_{max})$. This results in a total complexity for all p steps in C) together of $\mathcal{O}(p * q^2 * l_{max}) = \mathcal{O}(q^3 * l_{max})$.

The complexity of translating a CAR into the explicit representation (enumerating all solutions) is $\mathcal{O}((l_{max})^q)$, simply because there may be $\mathcal{O}((l_{max})^q)$ solutions for a query.

There are obviously many places where the algorithm above can be formulated more efficiently (order of inserting the U^i, cleaning, etc.). But for the purpose here it is enough to prove the result that queries are answered in linear time.

4   Conclusion

We introduced a linear time algorithm for evaluating Tree Matching problems, that returns complete answer representations (CARs) as answers. The algorithm employs a bottom-up strategy for index evaluation, what reduces the search space significantly. The notion of CARs helps to avoid the combinatorial explosion when evaluating Tree Matching queries.

A prototypical implementation of a system based on Indexed Tree Matching already exists. A future plan is to use a relational database system for the storage of nodes.

Future work of course includes expansion of the proposed algorithm to queries with don't care nodes. Another plan is the already insinuated formulation of frameworks as Constraint Satisfaction Problem, exploiting the different consistency techniques employed in this field.

A promising direction is the combination of other Information Retrieval models with structured documents in general and Indexed Tree Matching specifically. The IR model used here and by most other query models for structured documents is a simple Boolean model. But there are hints that Indexed Tree Matching can incorporate the vector space model, where it is possible to query about similarities of parts of documents.

Another rich field for future work is the communication with the user: How to present a CAR visually, and how to give the user the facility to refine her search.

Acknowledgements

I would like to thank Klaus Schulz for contribution of many ideas and interesting discussions on this work.

References

[Kil92] P. Kilpeläinen. *Tree Matching Problems with Applications to Structured Text databases*. PhD thesis, Dept. of Computer Science, University of Helsinki, 1992.

[KM93] P. Kilpeläinen and H. Mannila. Retrieval from hierarchical texts by partial patterns. In *Proc. ACM SIGIR'93*, pages 214–222, 1993.

[Loe94] A. Loeffen. Text databases: A survey of text models and systems. *SIGMOD Record*, 23(1):97–106, March 1994.

[NBY95] G. Navarro and R. Baeza-Yates. A language for queries on structure and contents of textual databases. In *Proc. ACM SIGIR'95*, pages 93–101, 1995.

[NBY96] G. Navarro and R. Baeza-Yates. Integrating contents and structure in text retrieval. *SIGMOD Record*, 25(1):67–79, 1996.

Combining the Power of Query Languages and Search Engines for On-line Document and Information Retrieval: The QIRi@D Environment

Laure Berti, Jean-Luc Damoiseaux, and Elisabeth Murisasco

GECT, Equipe Systèmes d'Information MultiMédia
Université de Toulon et du Var B.P. 132
83957 La Garde cedex, FRANCE
berti, jld, murisasco@univ-tln.fr

Abstract. In order to retrieve an item of information on the Web, many search engines have been proposed. They are rarely efficient at the first attempt: the display of results "forces" the user to navigate. In parallel, Web query languages have been developed to avoid these two sequential phases: research then navigation. In this context, the QIRI@D experimental platform, based on the functional programming language SgmlQL, enables both information retrieval and manipulation of distributed semi-structured documents published on a sub-network made up of the sites where QIRI@D is running. It is possible in an unique query to specify criteria to find a document, to filter it, to extract parts of it for building the result. An automatical enrichment of any published document is used to improve the search efficiency.

1 Introduction

The ever-widening growth of the "connected demography" on Internet significantly increases the number, the exchange and the circulation of networked documents. The World Wide Web is a fantastic mine of information with heterogeneous and unequal quality, but lots of documents are not worth of accessing. In a sens, it could be roughly considered as a huge non-administrated and only readable distributed database.

In order to retrieve a specific piece of information, many search engines are proposed ("classical" search engines, multi-search engines, generalized or specialized subject guides...) [17][10][3]. A Web search engine is a database of HTML documents gathered by a robot (program also called wanderer, crawler, spider, or bot...) and tools to generate and search it (with a combination of user-defined keywords and logical operators). Even if their common goal is to localize an item of information by retrieving the documents that match the keywords of the searcher, the way they manage to do it, is significantly different and depends on [15][12][3][2]:

1. the mode of documents collecting (the crop of documents is based on the authors' voluntary service (SubmitIt, Aliweb) and/or automatically generated by the robot which recursively retrieves linked pages and all documents that are referred),
2. the mode of documents indexing (manually or (semi)-automatically, full-text),
3. the pre-processing before the display of results (topics clusters, relevance scores to measure the quality of the match to the search query, duplicate detection),
4. the interface of display (control of the display format, user-defined Preferences, retrieval display options: limiting retrieval by field, manipulating the search set, saving and synthetically visualizing the results).

In spite of their resources, search engines are rarely efficient at the first attempt. End-users may increasingly rely on information professionals for complex searching. Actually, a query must always be specialized or generalized at the second or third attempt. And the original query must be modified in relation to the first list of proposed results by "relevance feedback". The user must adapt to the query syntax of the search engine he's using and to the successive refinements of the queries he has to elaborate. Anyway, the display of results (URL, summary, relevance score...) "forces" the user to navigate.

In parallel, Web query languages [8][9][13] have been developed to avoid these two phases (research then navigation) imposed by robots. Differents elements are essential in such a context:

1. unlike classical query languages which respect a precise data schema, the Web's user does not have any exact knowledge of the data structure within he searches information, neither of the structure of reached documents, query languages have to be adapted to this aspect [1][4][5][6],
2. otherwise, these languages have to consider the hypertextual aspect inherent in the Web structure,
3. finally, it is important to query the structure and/or the content of traversed nodes and to avoid invalid URLs.

To solve these difficulties, some languages propose original and specific solutions. Among them, WebSQL [13] and W3QL [9], SQL-like languages, integrate automatical and supervised navigation into queries, with or without access transparency to index servers for the user. Moreover, W3QL focuses on the extensibility of queries with users programs and UNIX's commands (such as grep, awk). It is also possible through a query to complete HTML forms encountered during navigation. By means of views, query results can be regularly refreshed. The relevant presentation of the results is another difficulty for query languages. A Datalog-like language, Weblog [8] proposes this original aspect: the restructuration of Web's parts. The user specifies in his query how results have to be presented.

We propose the QIRi@D environment: Quality and Information Retrieval in Electronic Documents, to combine the power of query languages and search engines. QIRi@D is an experimental platform enabling the manipulation of semi-structured documents (SGML and derived) wich are distributed and published on the administrated and controlled QIRi@D sub-network. This sub-network is made up of all the sites where QIRi@D is running. It is possible in a query to specify criteria to find a document, to filter it, to extract parts of it for building the result. The QIRi@D's programming language is SgmlQL [11]. It enables to query the structure and/or the content of documents and is currently extended to embed controlled navigation within a query, which constitutes the essential aspect on the Web.

This paper introduces the QIRi@D environment which proposes another solution for information search through distributed and semi-structured documents. The SgmlQL programming language is shortly recalled in Sect. 2. Sect. 3 details QIRi@D's local and distributed architecture. Sect. 4 and Sect. 5 present the pre-processing of a document and its manipulation within the QIRi@D environment. Conclusions and perspectives are given in Sect. 6.

2   SgmlQL: the Programming Language of QIRi@D

SGML (Standard Generalized Mark up Language)[7] is an international standard for the description of documents. It enables the tagging of document which determines the logical elements of its structure (chapters, sections, paragraphs). It is also possible to associate some attributes with logical elements to specify them independently of their content. The tagging of document is the only information added to text by means of markers defined in a grammar. This grammar is the core of a "Document Type Definition" (DTD) which represents the generic structure of that document. Notice that tags are not processing indications. So, the tagging makes easier not only the document manipulation but also its circulation and exchange through communication networks.

SgmlQL[11] is an SQL-like language for the manipulation of SGML documents. It is a functional language, an extension of OQL, an object oriented SQL language. SgmlQL has been defined to query SGML documents under any aspect whatever: tree-like structure, attributes, cross-references (hypertextual aspect). Note that SgmlQL directly queries SGML files without using a transcription of documents into a database schema, unlike other languages such as the one proposed by Christophides and al. in [4]. SgmlQL offers operators to browse and transform trees to extract document parts and to build new documents. These operators are embedded in each other such that `selectfromwhere`, `replace` or `remove`.

Moreover, SgmlQL[1] manipulates distributed documents through differents sites[14]. In this case, a first URL must be given. In order to briefly present the language, we give two typical queries:

```
Q1. Assignement of the file "Example.html" to the variable mybook.
global mybook = file "http://www.univ-tln.fr/Example.html" ;
```

During the whole session, the variable mybook can be used instead of the URL of file "Example.html".

```
Q2. What are the Title and the paragraphs of each section of mybook ?
element ANSWER
body :
   select [first TIT within s, select p from p in every PAR within s]
   from   s in every SEC within mybook;
```

For each section, its first title and all its paragraphs are extracted (the concatenation operator is noted "[ ]"). The result is a new SGML element (tag answer), its model content could be such as:

```
<!ELEMENT    Answer           (Title, Par)*              >
<!ELEMENT    Par              (#PCDATA | Bibref)+        >
<!ELEMENT    (Title|Bibref)   (#PCDATA)                  >
```

3   QIRi@D's Architecture

3.1   Overview

QIRi@D is a experimental platform to manage semi-structured, heterogeneous and distributed documents. It mainly provides the searching and the querying of SGML or HTML electronic documents and hyperdocuments. QIRI@D proposes (Fig. 1):

1. the enrichment of each document dedicated to the publishing,
2. the maintenance of the published documents,
3. the consultation of the published documents.

The use of QIRi@D respects the following principle: after the elaboration of a document, the author asks for publishing it in the QIRi@D network. Note that the user must respect a Charter to use the environment QIRi@D (normalized SGML, predefined tags, etc.). After the document publishing, any user who belongs to this network can exploit it. When a document is published, a set of information is extracted, calculated or inferred, to create a new richer document which will be the first target of any search. In a single formalism, user's exploitation combines a www-engine-like search function and the capacity to manipulate the retrieved document through its structure or/and its content.

---

[1] A complete definition of SgmlQL is available on-line in [16], where the language can be freely downloaded.

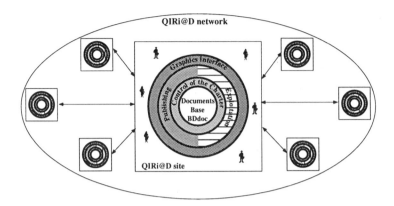

Fig. 1. General Architecture of a QIRi@D site

For example, it's possible to submit a query such as "for each document in St-Malo's server which contain information about buccaneers, extract all images available since january 1997".

QIRi@D runs on a site like a deamon based on the client-server principle. It's made up of tools written in SgmlQL shell and SGML files. The SGML files are built and manipulated by the tools which carry out the following tasks:

1. the publishing of document (enrichment, format control, etc.) ; the users of these services are called *Producers*,
2. the exploitation of document (structure and content manipulation, hyper-textual extension, etc.) ; the users of these services are called *Consumers*,
3. the system management.

3.2 BDdoc: the Local Document Base

The local documents base, called BDdoc, is made up of semi-structured documents in various format (SGML, HTML, Latex, RTF) published on this site. As it's shown in Fig. 2, its structure is locally distributed and composed by a set of *Producers* publishing directories (*user-docs*), and a main publishing directory (*system-doc*).

The publishing directory of the producer contains all the documents he wants to publish (*Primary Documents*). This directory is located on Producer login account, but it belongs to QIRi@D which manages it (the Producer can't have access to it). After the Producer asks for publishing (arrow 1 Fig. 2), QIRi@D effectively processes it (arrow 2 Fig. 2). Note, that a publishing operation is local on a QIRi@D site and must be expressed by an adherent of this site. The main publishing directory, managed by QIRi@D, usually contains:

1. all *Enriched Documents* made from the Primary Document processing ; an Enriched Document contains information about its quality and its history and other informations extracted, calculated or inferred from the Primary Document,
2. the index for all *Published Documents* and their localization.

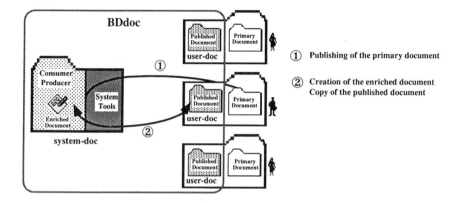

Fig. 2. BDdoc's Architecture

The indexes *Authors_Index* and *Information_Base_Index* (size, quality, modification frequency) won't be detailed in this paper. All these indexes define the structure of the BDdoc and they're stocked in a SGML document (*BDdoc.sgml*), which is an instance of this following DTD (Fig. 3) where the tag *Enriched_Doc* and the tag Form enable to reach through the "Href Attribute", respectively all Enriched Documents, authors information and access statistics (author consultation rate, document consultation rate, ...).

3.3 Distributed Base of the QIRi@D Network

The distributed base is evolutionary and open. It is distributed because it's made up of all Published Documents of all local bases of QIRi@D network (BDdocs) ; a Consumer has access in the same way to every document of the distributed base, even if it is local or distant. Evolutionary because, a Producer, who respects the Charter, can freely modify his Published Documents. It is open because a Producer can create a document which contains links with documents on other sites (adherent or not). However, the QIRi@D base contains a set of documents which are made from the Published Documents. These documents are locally bound to a site, and the Consumer don't have any access to them. They are used by QIRi@D to answer to the Consumer with the reached document.

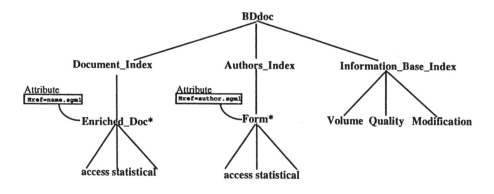

Fig. 3. BDdoc's Structure

4   Document Life Cycle and its Manipulation in the QIRi@D environment

The minimal Document Life Cycle in the QIRi@D environment starts with the Primary Document designed and produced by authors. Then, the system builds the corresponding Enriched Document which is the first target of any research query within the whole QIRi@D network. Precisely, the Document Life Cycle (Fig. 4) is based on four steps:

1. the conception of the Primary Document,
2. the local publishing of the Primary Document within its conception site, becoming now Published-Document
3. the creation of the unique associated Enriched Document,
4. the exploitation of the Enriched Document within and by the QIRi@D environment.

4.1   Conception of the Primary Document

A Primary Document is a tagged text in the SGML or HTML format, produced by authors with or without a WYSIWYG editor. In order to be publishable, this document will have to respect the QIRi@D Charter. That is, it will necessarily have to contain specific information integrated in predefined tags (such as authors' names, title and type of the document, ...). The Primary Document could be the root of hyper-documents. The Producer can attach in a separate file the corresponding DTD of the produced Primary Document. A strong constraint for the user to query the structure and the content of a document is to know its DTD.

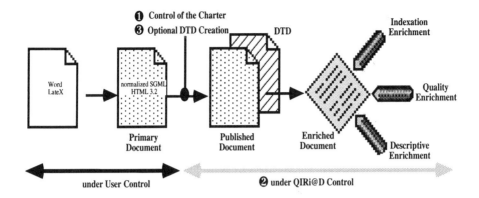

Fig. 4. From Raw Documents to Enriched Documents

4.2   Publishing of the Primary Document

When the Primary Document is designed and produced, its Producer can publish it on the site of his QIRi@D membership. If the Primary Document satisfies the set of constraints defined in the Charter, its publishing is possible: it becomes available on the whole QIRi@D network and for every member.

In the case of hyper-documents, the recursive path (following the local links) enables to determine the set of files intended to be published. The external links are not analyzed because the target documents are not local. The publishing of the Primary Document starts with verifying of the (non)-respect of the Charter (cf. 1 Fig. 4), especially about the main points:

1. at least one of the authors must be a QIRi@D member,
2. the tagging format must be respected (version 3.2 for HTML, closing tags are obligatory for SGML...),
3. the document must contain the predefined QIRi@D tags (title, author, keyword, category).

Then:

1. the component file(s) are moved in the user directory of publishing (cf. 2 Fig. 4),
2. the DTD of the Primary Document is automatically constructed (cf. 3 Fig. 4) if it has not been alreadyattached by the Producer,
3. the associated Enriched Document is elaborated,
4. *Information_Base_Index* is updated.

4.3   Creation of the Enriched Document

The Enriched Document is elaborated in adding information about the Published Document and it's an instance of the DTD shown in the Fig. 5which contain both generated information (e.g *DocId*) or extracted information about the Published Document (e.g as *Body*):

1. DocID is a SGML element, its content is an unique identifier affected to the Primary Document when it's published. The associated attributes are query results (cf. query Fig. 5) and store information about physical characteristics of the Primary Document (format, size, date),
2. the Primary-DTD is a SGML element, its attribute Href targets the document containing the DTD of the corresponding Primary Document ; this DTD is essential for the Consumer who will be able to make refined search on the document,
3. Body is a SGML element, its content is information extracted from the content of the Primary Document and which are likely to answer to general queries. Among the elements of its content:
   (a) the tag *Category* specifies the category of the document (article, course, ...),
   (b) the tag *Keyword* is a list of the keywords of the Primary Document,
   (c) the tag *Links* is a list of optional elements which contains for a Published Document the different URLs within the document(*Internal Link*), within the site (*Local Link*) and outside the local site (*External Link*).

Note, any Enriched document refers to its corresponding Published document, but is not its extented copy.

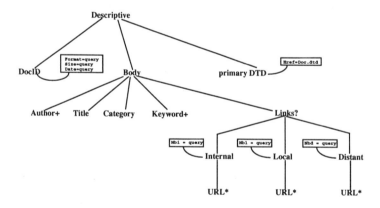

Fig. 5. Structure of an Enriched Document

4.4   Exploitation of an Enriched Document by QIRi@D

The QIRi@D environment proposes the twofold exploitation of Enriched Documents:

1. the consultation: a consumer queries the QIRi@D network from its membership site. The query is locally processed and if it's not sufficient (if the query doesn't concern the local site, or if the site/domain is unknown), it's subprocessed through of the QIRi@D network. Each site evaluates the query on all local base of Enriched Documents. If the answer to the query is found in the Enriched document, the corresponding Published Document is not reached. If the answer to the query is not found in the Enriched document, the corresponding Published Document is reached, thanks to the DocID tag of the Descriptive tag (cf. Fig. 5).

2. the maintenance of Published Documents by the system by mean of specific operators (update, delete). When a Producer wants to update a document that he has already published, he must modify the Primary Document and must publish it again with the same name: it is a new publishing. The associated Enriched Document is updated excluding its identifier. Its trace is updated. Only Producer can delete his own Published Documents. Then, QIRi@D deletes the associated Enriched Documents, updates informations of the local base (BDdoc), and finally deletes the Published Documents and their possible linked files (if they are hypertexts).

5   Consumer's Document Manipulation

This section illustrates a Consumer manipulation with the SgmlQL language. Assume that a Consumer searches all documents which deal with HTML on the Toulon's QIRi@D site. This Consumer wants to extract the title and the authors of each found document and expresses it with query Q1:

```
Q1: Title and Authors of documents dealing with HTML on Toulon's site
select  [first TIT within d , every AUT within d]              (1)
from    d in (every DOC within domain "univ-tln")             (2)
where   exists c in (every KEYWORD within d) : c match "HTML"  (3)
```

Line (2) builds the list of all the documents found on Toulon's site, and defines the variable d to browse that list. Line (3) checks, for each value of d – that is each document found – , whether its keywords match "HTML". Line (1) extracts for each value of d, the title of the current document and its authors. Actually, for an effective execution of that query, Toulon's QIRi@D environment locally applies the query Q1bis derived from Q1 on each Enriched Document of that site.

```
Q1bis : QIRi@D translation of Q1 query
select  [first TIT within file d->HREF, every AUT within file d->HREF] (1)
from    d in (every ENRICHED_DOC  within file "bddoc.sgml")           (2)
where   exists c in (every KEYWORD within file d->HREF):c match "HTML" (3)
```

The bddoc.sgml (cf. Fig. 3) document contains a set of tags ENRICHED_DOC (line 2). For each one of these tags, the attribute HREF is defined and its value is an URL of an Enriched Document. The content of each Enriched Document is reached and its keywords are compared with the string

"HTML" (line 3). The Consumer's query (line 1) extracts information through each one of these documents.

The four steps of Q1's evaluation are:

1. Q1 is locally typed by the consumer on his membership QIRi@D site,
2. the local SgmlQL interpreter analyses, optimises this query, and sends it to the concerned site(s) for its execution, in our example the "univ-tln" domain,
3. Q1 is then transformed into Q1bis on Toulon's site by the system,
4. the result of Q1bis is sent to the consumer's site.

6   Conclusion and Perspectives

We described in this paper the QIRi@D experimental platform for the management and the exploitation of semi-structured and distributed documents on QIRi@D network. Its implementation is in progress at present time. The system is entirely built upon the SgmlQL query language. The user is able, with a unique query, to use the same web-engines-like search function and to manipulate the retrieved and reached documents thanks to the automatical enrichment of documents elaborated by the QIRi@D system (about the structure and/or the content of documents, their hypertextual extension, their access history...).

In order to introduce new dimensions in the search and in the exploitation of on-line documents, our ongoing works focus the notion of enrichment concerning:

1. differents types of hypertextual links,
2. the data and document quality ; quality tags are integrated:
   (a) for extending the notion of relevancy-ranking[17][3] proposed by the search engines,
   (b) for personal and adaptative filtering of data and documents (user acquisition profile),

Moreover, the Producer will be able to add meta-information into his Primary Document during the conception step, to improve the indexation and the intrinsic quality of his document.

The main application of our environment is dedicated to Intranet applications.

References

1. S. Abiteboul, D. Quass, J. McHugh, J. Widow, J. Wiener,
   The lorel query language for semi-structured data,
   http://www.db.stanford.edu
2. L. Barlow, The Spider's Apprentice,
   http://www.monash.com/

3. K.Campbell,
   Tips on Popular Serach Engines,
   http://www.hamline.edu/library/bush/handouts/slahandout.html
4. V. Christophides, S. Abiteboul, S. Cluet, M. Schol,
   >From structured Documents to Novel Query Facilities,
   Proceedings of ACM-SIGMOD'94, Minneapolis (US), May 1994
5. C. Clifton, H. Garcia-Molina, D. Bloom,
   Hyperfile : a data and query model for documents,
   VLDB journal, 4, pp. 45-86, 1995
6. G. Gardarin, S. Yoon,
   HyWeb : un système d'interrogation pour le Web,
   Bases de Données Avancées (BDA' 96), Cassis 1996
7. C. F. Goldfarb,
   The SGML Handbook,
   Oxford Clarendon Press, 1990
8. L. V. S. Lakshmanan, F. Sadri, I. N. Subramanian,
   A declarative Language for querying and restructuring the Web,
   Proceedings of the Int. Workshop on Research Issues in Data Engineering
   (RIDE'96), New Orleans, 1996
9. D. Konopnicki, O. Shmueli,
   W3QS, a query system for the world-wide Web,
   Proceedings of the 21st VLDB Conference (VLDB'95), Zurich, Suisse 95
10. M. Koster,
   The Web Robots Pages,
   http://info.webcrawler.com/mak/projects/robots/robots.html
11. J. Le Maitre, E. Murisasco, M. Rolbert,
   SgmlQL, a language for querying SGML documents Proceedings of the 4th Euro-
   pean Conference on Information Systems (ECIS'96), Lisbon-Portugal, 1996
12. J. Liu,
   Understanding WWW Search Tools,
   http://www.indiana.edu/ librcsd/search/
13. A. O. Mendelzon, G.A. Mihaila, T. Milo,
   Querying the World Wide Web,
   Journal Digital Libraries, vol. 1, no. 1, 1997
14. P. Ramadour, E. Murisasco, J. Le Maitre ,
   Optimisation de requêtes mono-site et multi-sites,
   Rapport Interne no. 97-1, GECT, octobre 1997
15. W. D. Sullivan,
   A Webmaster's Guide To Search Engines,
   http://searchenginewatch.com/wgtse.htm
16. SgmlQL Manual,
   http://www.lpl.univ-aix.fr/projects/multext/mtsgmlql.html
17. R. Tyner,
   Sink or Swim : Internet Search Tools & Techniques,
   http://oksw01.okanagan.bc.ca/libr/connect96/search.htm

Intensional HTML

Bill Wadge, Gord Brown, m. c. schraefel, and Taner Yildirim

Department of Computer Science, University of Victoria
Victoria, B.C., V8W 3P6, CANADA
wwadge@csr.uvic.ca, gdbrown@csr.uvic.ca,
mc@csr.uvic.ca, taner_yildirim@pml.com

Abstract. Intensional HTML is a high-level Web authoring language that makes practical (using standard client and server software) the specification of pages and sites that exist in many different versions or variants.

Each page of IHTML defines an intension — an indexed family of actual (extensional) HTML pages which varies over a multi-dimensional author-specified version space. The version space is partially ordered by a refinement/specialization ordering. For example, `platform:mac` can be refined to `platform:mac+language:french` or to `platform:mac%k68` and the last two both refine to `platform:mac%k68+language:french`.

Authors can create multiple labeled versions of the IHTML source for a given page. Requests from clients specify both a page and a version, and the server software selects the appropriate source page and uses it to generate the requested actual HTML page.

Authors do not, however, have to provide separate source for each version. If the server-side software cannot find a source page with the exact version requested, it uses the page whose label most closely approximates the requested version. In other words, it treats the refinement ordering as a (reverse) inheritance ordering. Thus different versions can share source, and authors can write generic, multi-version code.

1 The Versioning Phenomenon

Many documents created for publication are produced in different variants or versions, corresponding, say, to different languages, different levels of expertise, different dates or different target audiences. In fact, most artifacts produced by humankind (documents or otherwise) appear in families of related versions, and the diversity in a family of documents (for example, user manuals) often simply reflects the corresponding diversity in a related family of more concrete entities.

The advent of the World Wide Web has, if anything, increased the pressure on authors to create multi-version documents, for a number of reasons. Firstly, the Web is international, and a truly international site must be available in many different languages. The bandwidth available to users varies greatly, so that some appreciate high quality graphics while others prefer purely text pages. Different browsers have different capabilities, for example, in terms of tables and frames. Some sites offer more material to paying subscribers while others may want certain information hidden from outsiders. Some sites would naturally offer different information (e.g. weather reports) to people in different parts of the world. Finally, site designers might want to offer sites that are customizable to take personal preferences (fonts, background colors) into account.

Furthermore, it seems at first sight that it should be easier to support on the web than in print mediums. Web documents are fetched on demand, in response to requests from individual users who could, if necessary, provide at the same time relevant personal information (such as language or level of expertise). In principle, server software could take these parameters as input and generate a made-to-measure version of the requested document.

In practice, however, there are very few sites which allow themselves to be reconfigured according to user preferences. In particular, there are very few truly multilingual sites. Even large international corporations, which typically provide multilingual versions of their front pages, soon revert to the "default" (i.e. English) version for their inner pages.

The problem lies with the very nature of HTML. HTML certainly allows pages to be generated on demand (through the CGI protocol) but provides no real support for authors who use it. CGI is an *escape* from HTML. Instead, authors usually stay with HTML and produce multi-version sites by cloning source files. Cloning works well in the short run, for a small number of versions, but breaks down when the version space is large and when the family of sites has to continue evolving.

In this paper we propose an alternate solution: we extend HTML to a (slightly) higher level language which allows users to specify families of sites without the user cloning or, in the current implementation, escaping through the CGI gate.

1.1   The Problem with Cloning

The easiest way to produce a variant of a web site is to make a copy of the HTML source and modify it. Unfortunately, the cloning (copying/modifying) approach to version creation can, in the long run, produce severe difficulties maintaining the resulting families of versions. The problems arise when changes are required in parts of the original that were copied unchanged into the new versions. The same changes have to be made many times, in the sources for all the versions which used the original code.

The inevitable result of the copy-and-modify approach is a large family of clones which, as a group, is almost impossible to change in any uniform way.

The obvious solution is ensure that the different members of the family share the *same* code (and not copies thereof) so that necessary changes are made only once and need not be propagated. To use Ted Nelson's terminology, we must arrange that different versions *transclude* the source they have in common.

This is easier said than done. In fact, exactly the same issues arise in the production of software (the documents being programs), and software version management is one of the most difficult problems in software engineering. Indeed, the success of the object oriented approach is due in part to class inheritance, which allows code to be shared (reused) on a large scale.

HTML certainly allows two different pages to link to a third, but this is a very crude form of sharing. Links are essentially pointers, and the problem with sharing via pointers is that you also share everything the shared object itself has pointers to.

Consider the problem of supporting English and French versions of a simple slide show. The slide show consists of a sequence of pages of text and/or graphics, each linked to the next page in the sequence. Obviously, we have to create separate English and French versions of pages with text on them. But we also have to make clones of any pages that have only images, even though the French and English versions will appear identical on the screen. The problem is that the English version of the page in question must be linked to the rest of the English version of the show, while the French version of the slide must be linked to the rest of the French version. Two separate source files are required.

2   The IHTML Solution

In this paper we present IHTML (Intensional HTML), an HTML-based authoring language which incorporates an object-oriented (inheritance based) approach to hypertext versioning. IHTML allows authors to define, with a single source file, a whole indexed family of HTML variants based on the file in question. These variants are generated on demand, then discarded after use. In a sense, IHTML automates the cloning process, and eliminates the maintenance problem by ensuring that the clones are short lived.

IHTML is *intensional* because IHTML source has both intensional and extensional meanings. The intension is the whole indexed family of HTML pages; the extensions are the different individual HTML pages.

The main feature of IHTML is that authors can provide multiple sources for the same page, each source labeled with a different version. The IHTML server-side software accepts requests for particular versions of particular pages, and generates the actual HTML from the appropriate IHTML source files.

For example, in the case of the slide show, the author could name the pages `slide1`, `slide2`, `slide3`, etc., and provide for each of these pages two source files, one English and one French.

IHTML authors do not, however, have to provide separate source files for every possible version. The IHTML index space ("version space") is partially ordered by a refinement relation, and the source for a more refined version is by default inherited from the less refined (more generic) versions.

When the server-side software receives a request for a particular version of a particular page (or part thereof), it looks for a source file labeled with the requested version. If there is no such source, it looks for a source file whose label most closely approximates the requested version (if there is no such source file, or no best source file, it reports an error). More refined versions can therefore by default transclude source from more generic ones, and a relatively small number of source files can define a very large family of pages.

For example, suppose that the fifth slide is purely graphical. The author can provide a *single* source file, labeled as the standard (so-called "vanilla") version. When a request comes for, say, the French version of page slide5, the server software first looks for a source file for that page labeled as the French version. When it finds none, it uses the more general standard version. Requests for the English version are similarly referred to the single standard source.

2.1 IHTML Links and Includes

Normally, links in IHTML source look exactly like links in ordinary HTML. They are interpreted, however, as denoting a whole family of links, each connecting a given version of the page they appear in to the *corresponding* version of the page they link to.

For example, suppose that the generic IHTML source for slide5 contains the link <a href=page6>next page</a>. This is interpreted as meaning that the English version of page5 is linked to the English version of page6, and that the French version of page5 is linked to the French version of page6. When the server software generates the French version of page5 from the generic source, it makes the generic link into a link to the French version of page6 (this might be the only change made).

IHTML also has a "server-side include" feature which causes the contents of an included file to be incorporated (by copying) into the HTML page under construction. For example, each page of the slide show might have <!-#include virtual=header -> at the top and <!-#include virtual=footer -> at the bottom, to include a standard header and footer in all slides. (The syntax was chosen to reflect the server-side include syntax of the Apache WWW server.)

The IHTML includes are also generic; for example, the English version of page4 will include the English version of the header. When processing an include, the server software looks for the version of the named source file whose version label most closely approximates the "current" version, i.e. the requested version of the file in which the include appears. Note that it looks for the *requested* version of the included file: the including page may exist in only a single, generic version, but a more specific version of the included file will be used if one can be found.

The include facility is very important for IHTML because it allows authors to break the source components into pieces smaller than a whole page. This allows the author to isolate the parts of a page that actually vary, and write more generic source for the parts (such as headers and footers) that do not. Conversely, the author may write generic source for a page as a whole, and include content which varies over whatever dimensions are appropriate.

2.2   The IHTML Version Space

The families of pages specified by IHTML are indexed by (subspaces of) the algebraically defined version space described in [1]. In the terminology of intensional logic [2], the elements of this space are *possible worlds*; each individual possible world (version) determines a particular extension, i.e. an actual HTML page.

The elements of the space described in [1] are expressions built up from identifiers using the operations + and %.

The % operator is the subversion operator: $V\%s$ is (by definition) a refinement of V. For example, Mac%k68 is a subversion of Mac.

The + operator is the version join operator: the least upper bound in the refinement ordering. Intuitively, version $V + W$ is the most general version which incorporates the modifications/refinements of *both* versions V and W. For example, the Mac%k68+french version might be the version which is designed for 68K Macs *and* uses French as its interface language.

Elements (versions) are partially ordered by a refinement operator: $\subseteq$. This operator can be read as "is refined by", or "is more general than". For example, $V \subseteq W$ says that W refines V, or that V is more general (closer to "vanilla") than W.

These ideas are formalized in the axioms presented in [1], for example:

$$V \subseteq V\%W \tag{1}$$

or

$$V\%(W_1 + W_2) = V\%W_1 + V\%W_2 \ . \tag{2}$$

The elements of this version space are equivalence classes of expressions together with the coarsest order which satisfies the axioms. This space is similar to Prolog's set of Herbrand terms: a convenient collection of abstract symbolic objects to which we can attach meanings.

The IHTML version space extends that of [1] in one important way: it allows explicit dimensions [3].

For example, we interpreted the term french in the above expression as referring to the French language. What if we were producing information about cooking and also needed to specify the cuisine? In the IHTML space, we can use arbitrary identifiers as dimensional "multipliers" and form sums that specify coordinates for each of the given dimensions. This enlarged space includes expressions such as

    platform:Mac%K68 + lang:french + cuisine:chinese .

The extra rules are:

$$D:\varepsilon \equiv \varepsilon \ , \tag{3}$$
$$D:(V + V') \equiv D:V + D:V' \ , \tag{4}$$
$$D:V \subseteq E:V' \leftrightarrow (D \equiv E) \text{ and } (V \subseteq V') \ . \tag{5}$$

(Here ε is the most general version: the standard or "vanilla" version.)

It should be clear now how to compare two dimension sums. In general:

$$D_0:V_0 + D_1:V_1 + \ldots \subseteq E_0:W_0 + E_1:W_1 + \ldots \tag{6}$$

if and only if for each D_i, either $V_i = \varepsilon$ or D_i is equal to E_j for some j and in that case $V_i \subseteq W_j$. (We assume that $D_i \neq D_j$ for $i \neq j$, and likewise for all E_i and E_j. In other words, there are no duplicates among the dimensions in a sum.)

2.3 Transversion Links

The second distinguishing feature of IHTML is the ability to define what we call *transversion* links. These are links that lead from the current version of the source page to a *different* version of the target page — different in a way specified in the tag. Transversion links allow visitors to the site to move from one version to another, without necessarily filling in forms or composing complex URLs. At the same time, they give the author full control over the way in which different versions of the site are interconnected.

A transversion link has the same format as an ordinary link, except that the tag may contain assignments to dimension identifiers. The link is interpreted as leading from a given version of the source page to the modified version of the target page — the modifications resulting from altering the coordinates of the given dimensions as specified.

For example, the author of the slide show might include, in the English versions of the source of the title page, a link of the form

```
<a href=page1 vmod="language:french"> .
```

In the (say) `language:english + background:blue` version of the title page, this will be interpreted as a link to the `language:french + background:blue` version of the first page. The "vmod" attribute defines a "version modifier" which is applied to the version of the current page.

Notice that following this link will take the reader to the French version of the whole slide show. The reason is that the French version of page 1 is linked to the French version of page 2, and so on. The English and French versions coexist as sort of parallel universes, and the transversion links let the reader move from one of these universes to the other.

IHTML also allows transversion includes, with a similar syntax. For example, `<!-#include virtual=footer.html vmod="language:english" ->` will include the footer in a version like the current version except that the `language` component is `english`.

IHTML also allows links to conventional (unversioned) HTML webware. We call these *extensional* (or *external*) links. One could think of an extensional link as a transversion link in which all the coordinates are set to ε. Accordingly, the syntax for an extensional link is `<a href=... version="">`. IHTML also has an extensional include tag.

2.4   IHTML with Existing Browsers

It might seem from what has been said that IHTML requires its own version of the server and client software. The requests from the client consist of a URL *and* a version. Satisfying such a request involves searching for the appropriate IHTML source file and then transforming the generic source into the particular HTML file corresponding to the version in question.

In fact, a prototype implementation of IHTML has been developed that uses existing browsers and existing server technology, by the author Yildirim (as part of his Master's thesis [4], completed June 1997). The basic idea is to ensure that all links to an IHTML-specified page go through a CGI script. The call to the script has two arguments, the generic URL and (a representation of) the particular version requested. The CGI script invokes the server-side software which locates the appropriate source file and produces the HTML.

The server software itself ensures that all links are CGI calls. When the software generates HTML from IHTML, it transforms the normal-looking generic IHTML links into CGI calls with the appropriate parameters. The first parameter, the URL, is taken directly from the IHTML source of the link. The second parameter, a version, is normally the same as the version included in the client request. In the case of a transversion link, however, the software modifies this version according to the information in the IHTML source of the link.

The CGI-based implementation proves that the basic concept works well, but it has some limitations. Performance is sometimes a problem, since there is non-trivial overhead in running a large CGI script for every HTTP request. In addition, URLs look strange to the user of the browser: everything starts with the same path (the path to the CGI script), and there is an unexpected numeric argument at the end of the URL. For these reasons (along with some implementation-level problems), authors Wadge and Brown have produced an entirely new implementation.

2.5   Current Implementation

The new version is an enhancement of the Apache WWW server [5]. Implemented as an Apache plug-in module, it traps HTTP requests for versioned entities (HTML pages, images, and so on), handling them separately, while letting requests for non-versioned things be handled by the server as usual. In this model, the user sees normal URLs, except that the name of a page has a version embedded in it. For example, a (partial) URL for the "language:turkish" version of page "zork.html" would be "zork.M1lw9qG3L4Bzjuee.html", given that "M1lw9qG3L4Bzjuee" is the encoding of "language:turkish". This version, although implemented as a modified server, still uses normal browser software (an essential feature, if the idea is to have any practical value whatsoever).

The implementation has three basic components: tools to aid the site designer in constructing a versioned site, software in the server to translate the URL in an HTTP request to a particular version of a particular filename, and software to translate IHTML source files to HTML.

Tools. The current tool set is Unix-based, consisting of modified "ls" and "cp" commands, as well as a front end to the "vi" text editor (or some other editor specified by the user). "icp" and "ivi" allow the user to specify the version of the file that is to be copied or edited; "ils" lists the versions in which an IHTML entity exists, in addition to the usual "ls" information. For example, to edit the language:english+graphics:lowres version of page zork.html, the site designer would use the command "ivi -v language:english+graphics:lowres zork.html". To list the available versions of the file, "ils zork.html". To copy an unversioned file alpha.html to the colour:blue version of zork.html, "icp -v colour:blue alpha.html zork.html".

URL to Filename Translation. Two steps in this process are different from the usual translation process. First, the software must decide whether the URL refers to a versioned object at all; if it doesn't, the IHTML component declines to handle the request, and processing continues normally. If it does, then the second step is to find the most relevant version of the requested file. If the exact version which was requested exists, it is chosen. If not, the software chooses the most relevant version (the maximum element of the set of less specific versions), assuming one exists. If none exists (the set has no unique maximum element, or there are no less specific versions), the usual HTTP "404" error is returned, indicating that the URL doesn't exist.

IHTML to HTML Translation. IHTML files may contain tags and/or tag attributes that must be transformed to standard HTML before files are sent to the browser. There are two basic transformations. First, a normal HTML tag, such as img, might have an attribute modified to include a version code: "src=pic.gif" becomes "src="pic.zj94kaz9zll-_a.gif"", supposing that "zj94kaz9zll-_a" is the representation of the version of interest. The modification will consider the current version of the page, as well as any version-modifying attributes present in the tag. Any tag attribute which refers to a file or URL is a candidate for modification. Second, any IHTML-specific tag will be replaced by whatever it indicates. For example, an include tag will be replaced by the appropriate version of the file named in its virtual attribute. With one exception, to be described shortly, text outside of tags is echoed verbatim to the browser.

Additional IHTML Features

Executable Includes. As with standard Apache server-parsed documents, IHTML files may include the output from the execution of arbitrary Unix programs (scripts or otherwise). The difference, naturally, is that IHTML executables may exist in multiple versions, with the appropriate version being chosen in the usual IHTML manner.

Explicit Versions. As well as links, includes, and so on which modify the current version of the page, it is also possible to specify the exact version of a link, include, or whatever. This feature is particularly useful when including links to other versioned sites, with version spaces different from that of the current site.

Structured Documents. HTML documents are already structured by their HTML tags, of course. However, IHTML allows a higher level of structure which describes which parts of a document to include in which versions. It behaves rather like a C-language "switch" statement: "If the current version is a refinement of version 'a', include the following IHTML fragment. If it is a refinement of version 'b', include this other fragment", and so on. This feature can save the site designer from creating many small files for minor variations of a file. Rather than, say, including a file which varies in the background dimension, to set the background colour for a document which doesn't otherwise vary in this dimension, the designer can simply specify a series of alternatives (based on the value of the background dimension) at the top of one file, which set the background colour to the appropriate value.

3   A Sample Intensional Site

Author Yildirim has produced a fairly elaborate multi-version home site (viewable using standard browsers) at URL

http://csr.uvic.ca/~taner/cgi-bin/scan.cgi .

(This site uses Yildirim's cgi-based implementation, but will soon be converted to run using the Apache-based implementation.)

At first sight, it looks like a fairly normal home page. One can follow links to related pages with Mr. Yildirim's biographical details, résumé, course work, and favorite bands and beers.

However, at the bottom of each of these pages is a link anchored to the phrase "*Turkish version of this site*". When we click it, the text on the page changes from English to Turkish.

The words are well chosen: if we proceed to explore the site again, we find the résumé, the course work, the bands and so on, but *all* these pages are in Turkish. We are now in the Turkish version of the whole *site*, not just of the home page. At the bottom there is an anchored phrase containing the words "*ingilizce versiyonu*" and, not surprisingly, it leads us back to the English version of the site.

Each page also offers us a similar transversion link to the text-only version (actually, versions) of the site.

Finally, on the home page there is a link anchored (in the English versions) to the phrase "*Background Options*". It takes us to a page with several small anchored images — background colors or patterns. Following, say, the link anchored to the orange square takes us to the home page of a version of the site in which *all* the pages have an orange background.

Note that we can view the different versions of the site with a standard browser, just by following links, without filling in forms or otherwise composing complex URLs. In fact, we do not need to know *anything* about the version algebra, including the fact that it exists at all.

The site described above uses an eight-dimensional version space. The dimensions are `language`, `display`, `background`, `date`, `category`, `order`, `text`, and `link`.

The `language` and `display` dimensions have two coordinate values each: `english`/`turkish` and `text`/`graphics`, respectively. In other words, the coordinate in the `language` dimension has either the value `english` or the value `turkish`, and the coordinate in the `graphics` dimension has either the value `text` or the value `graphics`.

The `background` dimension has thirty possible coordinate values and the `text` and `link` dimensions have twenty seven possible values.

Four distinct dates are used as the update dates.

The `category` dimension has six coordinate values: `humor`, `sports`, `music`, `movie`, `software`, `weather`.

The `order` dimension has two coordinate values: `ascending` and `descending`.

The site consists of thirteen intensional pages, each available in all versions — a total of more than 4.5 million virtual HTML pages (not every page varies in every version). The original one-version HTML program for the site consisted of about 38K bytes divided into 13 different files. The IHTML source consists of 192 files, but most of them, 94, are tiny files — consisting typically of a single line (such as `background=image/sky.gif` or `text="#FF00FF" link="#0000FF"`).

There is a total of 107K bytes of IHTML source — and most of the extra is Turkish versions of the original English text. These 107K bytes of IHTML source supports a virtual site which would correspond to over 13G bytes of cloned HTML.

4   Future Directions

The intensional approach to variation described here can be applied to any indexable family of pages, whether or not one might currently consider them to be "versions" of a single page.

For example, the slides in the slide show are obviously indexed by the natural numbers. We can therefore consider them to be variants of "the" slide, and add a `page_number` dimension to our version space. This would allow us to have a single generic IHTML source for all the slides, which would have headers, footers, logos, color choices etc. The generic slide page would include a `body` file, which itself would vary over the `page_number` dimension.

If we have a number of different slide presentations, we could in turn consider them to be versions of "the" presentation, and write an even more generic page for all our presentations.

At a university site, the pages for different departments could be produced as versions of a single generic department page that varies over the `department` dimension. Similarly, the different faculty pages could be treated as a family varying over a `professor` dimension.

A page which changes every day, e.g. that of a newspaper, can clearly be indexed by the set of dates. If we add a `date` dimension, we can write generic source which specifies parts of the layout (such as mastheads) that are invariant. We can extend our scheme by allowing source pages to be labeled by *intervals*, with the understanding that the source is valid for requests whose date coordinate lies in the interval. This idea is described in more detail in [6], where it is pointed out that it amounts to treating the Web as a kind of reactive system.

5   Aggregating Lists

In [7] author schraefel describes how the IHTML approach could be applied to a non-technical document — specifically, an essay on Wuthering Heights. The plan is to allow the reader to specify a set of parameters which identify the aspects of the essay in which they are particularly interested. They could specify a particular character, or that character's relation to a second character, an issue, degree of depth (from an abstract to a full essay) and a degree of documentation (from none, to complete footnotes and a full bibliography).

It soon became clear that early versions of IHTML would have difficulty with some aspects of this design, in particular the parameters that define intensities, and the specification of lists.

The problem with the original IHTML is that it is based on the standard object-oriented inheritance convention: given a request for a particular version of the page, we search for the most relevant (least generic) applicable source document. In forming a list, however, we want to pull in all (not just the most) relevant items.

As a result, both implementations of IHTML have a feature which allows a list to be formed by taking *all* relevant versions, not just the most relevant. In the latest implementation, this takes the particularly simple form of a variant of the C-like switch statement which concatenates *all* the bodies whose version conditions are relevant.

This simple extension could have many applications — consider how much of the information on the Web is composed of lists of some sort. With the aggregation extension, users can fine-tune the size and criteria for forming a list, and choose various formats for displaying it.

References

1. J. Plaice and W. W. Wadge, "A New Approach to Version Control", *IEEE Transactions on Software Engineering*, March 1993, pp268–276.
2. R. Thomason, editor, *Formal Philosophy, Selected Papers of R. Montague*, Yale University Press, 1974.
3. J. Plaice and S. Ben Lamine, "Eduction: A General Model for Computing", in E. A. Ashcroft, editor, *Intensional Programming II*, Singapore: World Scientific, 1997. In Press.
4. T. Yildirim, *Intensional HTML*, MSc Thesis, Computer Science Department, University of Victoria, 1997.
5. B. Behlendorf et.al, *The Apach HTTP Server Project*, httpd://www.apache.org/.

6. W. Wadge and A. Yoder, "The Possible-World Wide Web", in Mehmet A. Orgun, Edward A. Ashcroft, editors, *Intensional Programming I*, pages 207–213. Singapore: World Scientific, 1996. (also available at `http://lucy.uvic.ca/oo.html`).

7. m. c. schraefel, *Talking to Antigone*, PhD Dissertation (interdisciplinary), University of Victoria, 1997.

Data Model for Document Transformation and Assembly (Extended Abstract)

Makoto Murata[1]

Fuji Xerox Information Systems Co., Ltd., KSP 9A7, 2-1 Sakado 3-chome,
Takatsu-ku, Kawasaki-shi, Kanagawa-ken, Japan 213
murata@fxis.fujixerox.co.jp

Abstract. This paper shows a data model for transforming and assembling document information such as SGML or XML documents. The biggest advantage over other data models is that this data model simultaneously provides (1) powerful patterns and contextual conditions, and (2) schema transformation. Patterns and contextual conditions capture conditions on subordinates and those on superiors, siblings, subordinates of siblings, etc, respectively, and have been recognized as highly important mechanisms for identifying document components in the document processing community. Meanwhile, schema transformation has been, since the RDB, recognized as crucial in the database community. However, no data models have provided all three of patterns, contextual conditions, and schema transformation.

This data model is based on the forest-regular language theory. A schema is a forest automaton and an instance is a finite set of forests (sequences of trees). Since the parse tree set of an extended-context free grammar is accepted by a forest automaton, this model is a generalization of Gonnet and Tompa's grammatical model. Patterns are captured as forest automatons; contextual conditions are pointed forest representations (a variation of Podelski's pointed tree representations). Controlled by patterns and contextual conditions, an operator creates an instance from an input instance and also creates a reasonably small schema from an input schema. Furthermore, the created schema is often *minimally sufficient*; any forest permitted by it may be generated by some input instance.

1   Introduction

Document information, such as SGML or XML documents, is typically organized for particular purposes. However, the same information can be, if reorganized, utilized for different purposes. For example, Northwest may want to reorganize document information provided by Boeing and McDonnell-Douglas so as to efficiently maintain their airplanes in their own manner. Transformation and assembly of SGML/XML documents are expected to provide such reorganization, and have attracted strong interest in the SGML/XML community.

It is an exciting challenge to provide a data model for such transformation and assembly. Obviously, such models must capture ordered and heterogenous hierarchies of SGML/XML documents as well as the flexible schemas called DTD's

(Document Type Definitions). We further believe that such models must provide patterns and contextual conditions as well as schema transformation. Patterns and contextual conditions are well recognized in the document processing community, while schema transformation has been quite common in the database community. However, to the best of our knowledge, no data models have combined all three of patterns, contextual conditions, and schema transformation simultaneously.

Patterns and contextual conditions help to identify interesting or useful nodes in SGML/XML documents. In our terminology, a *pattern* is a condition on (immediate or non-immediate) subordinate nodes. For example, given PODDP'98 papers, we might want to retrieve sections containing the word "preliminaries" in their titles. Here a pattern is *containing sections whose titles contain "preliminaries"*. In our terminology, a *contextual condition* is a condition on non-subordinates such as (immediate or non-immediate) superiors, siblings, and subordinates of siblings, etc. For example, assume that we are interested only in those sections of document database papers. Then, we want to introduce a contextual condition: *the section must be directly or indirectly subordinate to a paper node such that its title node contains the word "document"*. Many SGML/XML transformation engines[1] support such patterns and contextual conditions. Academic papers on document retrieval via patterns and contextual conditions are surveyed by Baeza-Yates and Navarro [3].

On the other hand, many data models provides schema transformation. For example, the projection operator of the RDB not only creates an instance (a set of tuples) but also a schema, which is a schema with fewer attributes. The created instance is guaranteed to conform to the created schema, although the schema is constructed only from the input schema (without considering the instance). Schema transformation is highly important for at least two reasons. First, a programmer can combine operators repeatedly, since he or she knows the intermediate schema created by each operator. He or she only has to make sure that the next operator is applicable to this intermediate schema. Second, queries designed for a database schema are applicable to any database instance of this schema. The instance returned by the query conforms to the schema created from the database schema.

We believe that schema transformation combined with patterns and contextual conditions will become extremely important for document transformation and assembly. For example, if our operator renames top-level *segments* as *chapters*, the created schema should allow *chapters* as top-level components only and allow *segments* as non-top-level components only. (Here "top-level *segments*" is a contextual condition.) If our operator renames lowest-level *segments* as *topics*, the created schema should allow *topics* as the lowest-level components only. (Here "lowest-level *segments*" is a pattern.) Such schemas allow documents to be transformed and assembled repeatedly. To the best of our knowledge, none of the existing data models provides such schema transformation.

---

[1] See http://www.sil.org/sgml/publicSW.html#conversion.

On the basis of the forest-regular language theory [11, 13] (a branch of the tree automaton theory [7]), we present a new data model that combines patterns, contextual conditions, and schema transformation. A forest is an ordered sequence of trees. A schema is a forest automaton and an instance is a finite set of forests. A pattern is captured by a forest automaton; a contextual condition is captured by a pointed forest representation (a variation of pointed tree representations [12]). Given a query based on a pattern and contextual condition, we can construct a reasonably small schema. In many cases, the constructed schema is *minimally sufficient*; any forest permitted by this schema may be generated from some input instance.

The mathematically clean properties of forest-regular languages help to develop an equivalent algebra and rule-based language. First, the class of forest-regular languages is closed under boolean operations. Along with the fact that an instance is a set of forests rather than a single forest, this closure property provides boolean operators readily. Second, this class is also closed under concatenation and root removal. This closure property provides forest composition and decomposition operators. (Observe that we would lose this property if we used trees rather than forests.) Furthermore, our algebra can easily mimic the relational algebra and any query is in PTIME, although we defer the proof to the full paper for space limitation.

The rest of this paper is organized as follows. Section 2 discusses related work on document database systems. Section 3 introduces forests and forest automatons, and then defines schemas and instances. Sections 4 presents an algebraic language called the forest algebra, and Section 5 demonstrates two examples of document transformation. Section 6 presents a rule-based language called forestlog.

2 Related Work

There have been a number of data models for structured documents, and they are surveyed by Baeza-Yates and Navarro [3]. Most of these models concentrate on retrieval rather than transformation and assembly. Furthermore, little attention has been paid to schema transformation combined with patterns and contextual conditions.

Regarding those works which provide schema transformation, there have been two approaches. One approach uses complex value models [2] or object-oriented models [14]. The other approach [6, 8, 9] uses grammars and parse trees.

Complex value models extend the relational data model by allowing sets and nesting of sets and tuples. Other constructors such as bags and lists are often introduced. Object-oriented models further extend complex value models by introducing OID's, class hierarchies, methods, etc. Both types of models provide algebras, calculus, and rule-based languages, which are equally expressive. They are elegant extensions of the relational algebra, the relational calculus, and datalog, respectively.

Several attempts have been made to capture hierarchies of structured documents with complex value models or object-oriented models. Probably, the most notable example is by Christophides *et al.* [5]. They use O_2 as a basis and further introduce ordered tuples and marked unions so as to capture hierarchies of SGML/XML documents. However, as a result of combining these mechanisms, the representation of a hierarchy becomes complex. For example, the sibling relationship is hard to utilize, as marked unions and OID's intrude. Furthermore, modifications to a DTD, even when the new DTD permits all documents permitted by the current DTD, lead to cumbersome update of database instances. This model introduces contextual conditions on ancestors, but schema transformation does not take full advantage of them, thus providing loose schemas.

An entirely different approach provides grammatical models ([1, 6, 8, 9] among others). A schema in a grammatical model is an extended context-free grammar. An instance of this schema is a derivation tree. This approach naturally captures SGML/XML documents. However, none of the existing models provides schema transformation combined with patterns and contextual conditions. Gonnet and Tompa [8] provide powerful operators, but the result of a query does not have an associated schema. Further, no declarative query languages are provided. Abiteboul, Cluet, and Milo [1] provide schema transformation, but do not provide schema transformation combined with patterns and contextual conditions. Gyssens *et al.* [9] provide an equivalent algebra and calculus, but both are complex and operators are too primitive. Neither their algebra nor calculus are natural extensions of the RDB. Weak patterns are provided, but contextual conditions are not. Colby *et al.* [6] provide a powerful algebra, but does not provide declarative languages. This algebra is not a natural extension of the RDB. Patterns are rather powerful, but contextual conditions are weak. Schema transformation and patterns are combined , but the created schemas tend to be loose (i.e., they allow unnecessary documents).

3   Schemas and Instances

In preparation, we define forests and forest automatons. Let Σ be a finite set of symbols and let X be a finite set of variables. We assume that Σ and X are disjoint and they do not contain $\langle$ or $\rangle$.

A *forest* over Σ and X is a string $(\in (\Sigma \cup X \cup \{\langle, \rangle\})^*)$ of the forms as below:

- ϵ (the null forest),
- x ($x \in X$),
- $a\langle u\rangle$ ($a \in \Sigma$, and u is a forest), or
- uv (u and v are forests).

Examples of forests are $a\langle x\rangle$, $a\langle \epsilon\rangle\, b\langle b\langle \epsilon\rangle\, x\rangle$, and $a\langle \epsilon\rangle\, b\langle x\, b\langle b\langle \epsilon\rangle\, x\rangle\, c\langle \epsilon\rangle\rangle$. Observe that symbols in Σ are used as labels of non-leaf nodes of forests and that variables in X are used as those of leaf nodes.

The set of forests over Σ and X is denoted by $\mathbf{F}[\Sigma, X]$. A *tree* is a forest of the form $a\langle u\rangle$. We abbreviate $a\langle \epsilon\rangle$ as a. Thus, the second example is abbreviated as $a\, b\langle b\, x\rangle$.

A *deterministic forest automaton* (DFA) M over a finite set Σ and a finite set X (disjoint from Σ) of variables is a 4-tuple $<Q, \iota, \alpha, F>$, where:

- Q is a finite set of states,
- ι is a function from X to Q,
- α is a function from $\Sigma \times Q^*$ to Q such that for every $q \in Q$ and $x \in \Sigma$, $\{q_1 q_2 \ldots q_k \mid k \geq 0, \alpha(a, q_1 q_2 \ldots q_k) = q\}$ is regular, and
- F is a regular set (called the *final state sequence set*) over Q.

Given a forest in $\mathbf{F}[\Sigma, X]$, we execute M in the bottom-up manner. First, we assign a state to every leaf node that is labeled with a variable. This is done by computing $\iota(x)$, where x is the variable. Then, we repeatedly assign a state to every node whose subordinate nodes have assigned states. This is done by computing $\alpha(a, q_1 q_2 \ldots q_k)$, where a is the label of the node and $q_1 q_2 \ldots q_k$ is the sequence of states assigned to the subordinate nodes. Consider the top-level nodes in the given forest and the sequence of those states assigned to them. If this state sequence is an element of the final state sequence set, that forest is *accepted* by M.

The *language accepted* by M, denoted $L(M)$, is the set of forests accepted by M. If a set of forests is accepted by some DFA, this set is *forest-regular*. As in the string case, there are non-deterministic forest automatons and forest-regular expressions. Almost all of the clean properties of regular languages apply to forest-regular languages.

Before we define schemas and instances, we have to consider one difference between the automaton theory and database theory. Although our Σ and X are both finite, the database theory uses countably infinite sets. For example, the RDB theory typically uses a countably infinite set **label** for attributes. Specific RDB schemas or instances use only finite subsets of **label**, but one may introduce new symbols at any time as **label** is countably infinite. The RDB theory uses another countably infinite set **dom**, which contains constants such as integers or strings. An RDB instance has such constants as attribute values.

We follow the database theory approach and use two countably infinite sets **label** and **dom**. They are disjoint and do not contain $\langle$ or $\rangle$. In the SGML/XML terminology, **label** is the set of names and **dom** is the set of character data.

Accordingly, we extend the definition forests. A forest over **label** and **dom** is a string ($\in \mathbf{label} \cup \mathbf{dom} \cup \{\langle, \rangle\})^*$) of the forms as below:

- ϵ (the null forest),
- x ($x \in \mathbf{dom}$),
- $a\langle u \rangle$ ($a \in \mathbf{label}$, and u is a forest), or
- uv (u and v are forests).

The sets of forests over **label** and **dom** is denoted by $\mathbf{F}[\mathbf{label}, \mathbf{dom}]$.

In the database theory, a special symbol $t (\notin \mathbf{label} \cup \mathbf{dom})$ is typically used in schemas as place holders for constants. An instance of this schema is a finite set of objects that can be obtained by replacing t with constants in **dom**.

We also use a special symbol t for representing schemas. Symbol t is comparable to #PCDATA of SGML/XML. Keyword #PCDATA occurs only in DTD's, and do not occur in documents. Documents contain character data when the corresponding portion of the DTD is #PCDATA.

Now, we are ready to define schemas and instances. A *schema* is a DFA M over a finite subset of **label** and a singleton $\{t\}$. Two schemas are *equivalent* if they accept the same language. An *instance* over M is a finite subset I of **F[label, dom]** such that each forest in I is obtained from some forest in $L(M)$ by replacing t with constants in **dom**; difference occurrences of t need not be replaced with the same constant. Note that an instance is not a forest but rather a set of forests. A *database schema* is a collection of schemas $\{M_1, M_2, \ldots, M_m\}$. A *database instance* over this database schema is a collection $\{I_1, I_2, \ldots, I_m\}$, where I_i is an instance of M_i.

4   Forest Algebra

We recursively define *queries*. Let q_1 and q_2 be queries, and let a be a label in **label**. The value of q_1 is denoted $I(q_1)$ and the schema of q_1 is denoted $M(q_1)$. Value $I(q_1)$ is an instance of $M(q_1)$. Observe that schema DFA's can be effectively constructed for all operators.

Basic Values: A variable denoting an (extensional) instance of some schema M is a query. The value is that instance and the schema is M.

Constant values: For every constant c in **dom**, $\{c\}$ is a query. The schema is a DFA that accepts $\{t\}$.

Basic set operations: $q_1 \cap q_2$, $q_1 \cup q_2$, and $q_1 - q_2$ are queries. Their values are defined in the obvious manner. The schemas of $q_1 \cap q_2$ and $q_1 \cup q_2$ are DFA's that accept $L(M(q_1)) \cap L(M(q_2))$ and $L(M(q_1)) \cup L(M(q_2))$, respectively. The schema of $q_1 - q_2$ is $M(q_1)$.

Forest composition and decomposition operations:

- **concat**(q_1, q_2) and **addroot**(a, q_1) are queries. These operators come from the definition of terms. The values are $\{u_1 u_2 \mid u_1 \in I(q_1), u_2 \in I(q_2)\}$ and $\{a\langle u\rangle \mid u \in I(q_1)\}$, respectively. The schema DFA's accept $\{u_1 u_2 \mid u_1 \in L(M(q_1)), u_2 \in L(M(q_2))\}$ and $\{a\langle u\rangle \mid u \in L(M(q_1))\}$, respectively.
- q_1/q_2, $q_1\backslash q_2$, and **removeroot**(a, q_1) are queries. These operators are destructors corresponding to the above constructors.
  The values are $\{v \mid u_1 = vu_2, u_1 \in I(q_1), u_2 \in I(q_2)\}$, $\{v \mid u_1 = u_2v, u_1 \in I(q_1), u_2 \in I(q_2)\}$, and $\{u \mid a\langle u\rangle \in I(q_1)\}$, respectively. The schema DFA's accept $\{v \mid u_1 = vu_2, u_1 \in L(M(q_1)), u_2 \in L(M(q_2))\}$, $\{v \mid u_1 = u_2v, u_1 \in L(M(q_1)), u_2 \in L(M(q_2))\}$, and $\{u \mid a\langle u\rangle \in L(M(q_1))\}$, respectively
- **subtree**(q_1) is a query. This operator retrieves subtrees. It can be compared to the powerset operator in complex object models, although our operator does not require exponential time.

The value is the set of all trees v such that v is a subtree of some element in $I(q_1)$. The schema is a DFA that accepts $\{v \mid v$ is a subtree of $u, u \in L(M(q_1))\}$.

- **prod**(a, q_1, q_2) is a query. This operator constructs higher forests. It comes from the definition of forest-regular expressions, which is beyond the scope of this paper.

  The value is the set of all forests v for which there exist $u_1 \in I(q_1)$ and $u_2 \in I(q_2)$ such that v is obtained by replacing each occurrence of a as a leaf in u_1 by u_2. Different occurrences of a must be replaced with the same forest [2].

  The schema is a DFA that accepts the set of all forests v for which there exists $u_1 \in L(M(q_1))$ such that v is obtained by replacing each occurrence of a as a leaf in u_1 by some element in $L(M(q_2))$.

- **rewrite**(a, i, v, q_1) and **genrewrite**(a, v', q_1) are queries, where i is a non-negative integer, v is a forest over **label** and **dom** $\cup \{\mu_1, \mu_2, \ldots, \mu_i\}$, and v' is a forest over **label** and **dom** $\cup \{\mu_1, \mu_2\}$. These operators rewrite forests and are variations of tree homomorphisms [7].

  The value of **rewrite**(a, i, v, q_1) is the set of forests in $I(q_1)$ rewritten with a, i, v. Each node in a forest is replaced with v, if the label of the node is a and the number of its subordinates is i. The result of rewriting the j-th subtree of the node is assigned to variable μ_j in v $(1 \le j \le i)$. Likewise, the value of **genrewrite**(a, v, q_1) is the set of forests in $I(q_1)$ rewritten with a, v. Each node in a forest is replaced with v if the label of the node is a. The result of rewriting the subordinates is assigned to variable μ_1 and the mirror image of that result is assigned to variable μ_2.

  As the schemas of **rewrite**(a, i, v, q_1) and **genrewrite**(a, v, q_1), we would like to construct DFA's that accept $\{\mathbf{rewrite}(a, i, v, u) \mid u \in L(M(q_1))\}$ $\{\mathbf{genrewrite}(a, v, u) \mid u \in L(M(q_1))\}$, respectively. Unfortunately, this is not always possible, since these sets are not always forest-regular. (Just like $\{p^n q p^n \mid n = 1, 2, \ldots\}$ is not regular.) However, we can construct larger but reasonably small DFA's. (Just like we can construct a string automaton that accepts $\{p^m q p^n \mid m, n = 1, 2, \ldots\}$.) Such construction is given by Gécseg and Steinby [7].

Operators based on patterns and contextual conditions:

- **select**(M, q_1) is a query, where M is a deterministic DFA over a finite subset of **label** and a finite subset of **dom** $\cup \{t, \mu\}$. This operator comes from the RDB and pattern matching.

  The value of **select**(M, q_1) is the set of all u in $I(q_1)$ such that u can be obtained from some forest in $L(M)$ by replacing t and μ with constants. Different occurrences of t need not be replaced with the same constant.

---

[2] Forest regular expressions actually differ from our **prod** operator in that different occurrences of a need *not* be replaced with the same forest. Our operator is designed so that it can be mimicked by our rule-based language *forestlog*.

Meanwhile, all occurrences of μ must be replaced with the same constant, thus providing equality conditions.

The schema of **select**(M, q_1) is a DFA that accepts $L(M(q_1)) \cap \{f(u) \mid u \in L(M)\}$, where f is a projection that replaces μ and constants with t.

– **mark**$(a, \mathcal{C}, \mathcal{P}, q_1)$ is a query, where a is a label in **label**, $\mathcal{C}$ is a contextual condition (see below), and $\mathcal{P}$ is a pattern (see below). The role of this operator is to locate nodes that satisfy patterns and contextual conditions and then rename these nodes.

This operator is the most complicated in our algebra, but is also the source of its expressiveness. We introduce this operator only informally. Our previous paper [10] shows a formal definition, the algorithms for pattern matches and contextual condition testing, and the effective construction of an output schema ([10] is restricted to binary tress though).

In preparation, we study pointed forests and pointed forest representations (a variation of pointed trees and pointed tree representations [12]). A *pointed forest* over a finite alphabet Σ and a finite set X of variables is a forest over Σ and X such that one node is special and that its subordinates is the null forest. For example, $p\dot{q}r$ and $p\langle\dot{q}r\rangle$ are pointed forests, where $\dot{q}$ is a special node. (Remember that q is an abbreviation of $a\langle\epsilon\rangle$.) A *pointed base forest* is a pointed forest such that its special node is a top-level node. A pointed forest is uniquely decomposed into a sequence of pointed base forests. For example, $p\langle qxr\langle\dot{s}yt\rangle\rangle u$ is uniquely decomposed into $\dot{s}yt, qx\dot{r}, \dot{p}u$.

A *pointed base forest representation* is a triplet (L_1, a, L_2), where L_1, L_2 are forest-regular languages over Σ and X, and a is a symbol in Σ. A set of pointed base forests $\{u_1\dot{a}u_2 \mid u_1 \in L_1, u_2 \in L_2\}$ is represented by (L_1, a, L_2). A *pointed forest representation* is a regular expression over a finite set of pointed base forest representations. The represented language is the set of pointed forests w such that the decomposition of w, which is a sequence of pointed base forests, can be derived from the regular expression and pointed base forest representations. For example, $(\mathbf{F}[\Sigma, X], p, \mathbf{F}[\Sigma, X])^*$ represents the set of pointed forests such that the special node and all its superiors are labeled with p.

A *contextual condition* $\mathcal{C}$ is a pointed forest representation over a finite subset of **label** and a finite subset of **dom** $\cup \{t\}$. The *envelope* of a node in a forest is the result of removing the subordinates of that node and making the node special. A node in a forest *satisfies* a contextual condition if the envelope of that node is obtained from some element of $L(\mathcal{C})$ by replacing occurrences of t with constants in **dom**.

A *pattern* $\mathcal{P}$ is a pair of (1) a DFA M over a finite subset of **label** and a finite subset of **dom** $\cup \{t\}$, and (2) a strongly unambiguous regular expression e that represents the final state sequence of M. (For any string, there is at most one way to generate this string from a strongly unambiguous regular expression. For example, p^* is strongly unambiguous, but $(p^*)^*$ is not.) Some subexpressions of e, including e itself, have associated labels in **label**. A node *matches a pattern* if the subordinate forest of that node is obtained from some forest in $L(M)$ by replacing t with constants in **dom**.

Now, let us define the value of **mark**$(a, \mathcal{C}, \mathcal{P}, q_1)$. It is the set of forests that are derived from some forest in $I(q_1)$ as follows: for every node that satisfies $\mathcal{C}$ and matches $\mathcal{P}$, we relabel that node with a and introduce nodes corresponding to labeled subexpressions of strongly unambiguous regular expression e. Each of these nodes has the label associated with the corresponding subexpression.

5   Transformation Examples

This section shows two examples of document transformation. Observe that our queries provide not only database instances but also schemas. The first example demonstrates that our algebra has realistic applications. The second example demonstrates that our schema transformation takes full advantage of patterns and contextual conditions.

5.1   Manipulation of Dictionary Entries

This example is inspired by the OED shortening project [4]. We would like to extract interesting entries of a dictionary. Every entry is represented by an SGML document that conforms to a DTD as below:

```
<!ELEMENT ENTRY       (HEADLINE,SENSE*)>
<!ELEMENT HEADLINE    (#PCDATA)>
<!ELEMENT SENSE       (DEFINITION,QUOTE*)>
<!ELEMENT DEFINITION  (#PCDATA)>
<!ELEMENT QUOTE       (AUTHOR?,TEXT)>
<!ELEMENT AUTHOR      (#PCDATA)>
<!ELEMENT TEXT        (#PCDATA)>
```

We consider each entry as a forest and the dictionary as an instance. We first construct a schema DFA from the above DTD, but we do not present it for space limitation.

We would like to retrieve all entries that contain quotations from Shakespeare. This is done by a query **select**(M, z), where z is a variable representing the original dictionary. Pattern M is a deterministic forest automaton $<\{r_0, r_1, r_2\}, \kappa, \beta, L((r_0|r_1|r_2)^* r_2 (r_0|r_1|r_2)^*)\}>$ over Σ and $\{t, \text{"Shakespeare"}\}$ ("Shakespeare" $\in$ **dom**), where

$$\Sigma = \{\texttt{ENTRY, HEADLINE, SENSE, DEFINITION, QUOTE, AUTHOR, TEXT}\},$$

$$\kappa(x) = \begin{cases} r_0 & (x = t) \\ r_1 & (x = \text{"Shakespeare"}), \text{ and} \end{cases}$$

$$\beta(a, u) = \begin{cases} r_2 & (a = \texttt{AUTHOR}, u = r_1) \\ r_2 & (u \in L((r_0|r_1|r_2)^* r_2 (r_0|r_1|r_2)^*)) \\ r_0 & (\text{otherwise}) . \end{cases}$$

Other than a shortened dictionary (a set of forests), this query constructs a schema DFA for shortened dictionaries. A minimum DTD constructed from this DFA is as below:

```
<!ELEMENT ENTRY       (HEADLINE,SENSE+)>
<!ELEMENT HEADLINE    (#PCDATA)>
<!ELEMENT SENSE       (DEFINITION,QUOTE*)>
<!ELEMENT DEFINITION  (#PCDATA)>
<!ELEMENT QUOTE       (AUTHOR,TEXT)>
<!ELEMENT AUTHOR      (#PCDATA)>
<!ELEMENT TEXT        (#PCDATA)>
```

5.2 Renaming Top-Level and Bottom-Level Segments

Consider documents containing segments. Each segment contains a title and some paragraphs, and also contains segments recursively. We want to rename top-level segments as sections and lowest-level segments as topics. As in the previous example, we would like to transform not only documents but also schemas.

Our schema is a DFA $<Q, \iota, \alpha, F>$ over Σ and $\{t\}$, where:

$$\Sigma = \{\mathsf{Doc}, \mathsf{Seg}, \mathsf{Ttl}, \mathsf{Par}\},$$
$$Q = \{q_{\mathsf{doc}}, q_{\mathsf{seg}}, q_{\mathsf{ttl}}, q_{\mathsf{par}}, q_t, q_{\mathsf{deadend}}\},$$
$$\iota(t) = q_t,$$
$$\alpha(a, u) = \begin{cases} q_{\mathsf{doc}} & (a = \mathsf{Doc}, u \in L(q_{\mathsf{seg}}^*)) \\ q_{\mathsf{seg}} & (a = \mathsf{Seg}, u \in L(q_{\mathsf{ttl}} q_{\mathsf{par}}^* q_{\mathsf{seg}}^*)) \\ q_{\mathsf{ttl}} & (a = \mathsf{Ttl}, u = q_t) \\ q_{\mathsf{par}} & (a = \mathsf{Par}, u = q_t) \\ q_{\mathsf{deadend}} & (\text{otherwise}), \text{ and} \end{cases}$$
$$F = \{q_{\mathsf{doc}}\} \ .$$

and an equivalent DTD is as below:

```
<!ELEMENT Doc  (Seg*)>
<!ELEMENT Seg  (Ttl, Par*, Seg*)>
<!ELEMENT Ttl  (#PCDATA)>
<!ELEMENT Par  (#PCDATA)>
```

First, we rename top-level segments as sections by the **mark** operator. Our contextual condition is a pointed forest representation $(\mathbf{F}[\Sigma, \{t\}], \mathsf{Doc}, \mathbf{F}[\Sigma, \{t\}])$ $(\mathbf{F}[\Sigma, \{t\}], \mathsf{Seg}, \mathbf{F}[\Sigma, \{t\}])$. Our pattern is a minimum DFA that accepts $\mathbf{F}[\Sigma, \{t\}]$ and a strongly unambiguous regular expression representing the final state sequence of this DFA.

Second, we rename lowest-level segments as topics by the **mark** operator again. Our contextual condition is a pointed forest representation $(\mathbf{F}[\Sigma, \{t\}], \mathsf{Doc}, \mathbf{F}[\Sigma, \{t\}])(\mathbf{F}[\Sigma, \{t\}], \mathsf{Seg}, \mathbf{F}[\Sigma, \{t\}])^*$. Our pattern is a minimum

DFA that accepts $\mathbf{F}[\Sigma - \{\mathsf{Seg}\}, \{t\}]$ and a strongly unambiguous regular expression representing the final state sequence of this DFA.

Other than a set of transformed documents, these operators create a schema DFA $<Q', \iota', \alpha', F'>$ over Σ' and $\{t\}$, where:

$$\Sigma' = \{\mathsf{Doc}, \mathsf{Seg}, \mathsf{Ttl}, \mathsf{Par}, \mathsf{Sec}, \mathsf{Tpc}\},$$

$$Q' = \{q_{\mathrm{doc}}, q_{\mathrm{seg}}, q_{\mathrm{ttl}}, q_{\mathrm{par}}, q_{\mathrm{sec}}, q_{\mathrm{tpc}}, q_t, q_{\mathrm{deadend}}\},$$

$$\iota'(t) = q_t,$$

$$\alpha'(a, u) = \begin{cases} q_{\mathrm{doc}} & (a = \mathsf{Doc}, u \in L(q_{\mathrm{sec}}^*)) \\ q_{\mathrm{sec}} & (a = \mathsf{Sec}, u \in L(q_{\mathrm{ttl}}\, q_{\mathrm{par}}^*\, (q_{\mathrm{seg}}|q_{\mathrm{tpc}})^*)) \\ q_{\mathrm{seg}} & (a = \mathsf{Seg}, u \in L(q_{\mathrm{ttl}}\, q_{\mathrm{par}}^*\, (q_{\mathrm{seg}}|q_{\mathrm{tpc}})^*)) \\ q_{\mathrm{tpc}} & (a = \mathsf{Tpc}, u \in L(q_{\mathrm{ttl}}\, q_{\mathrm{par}}^*)) \\ q_{\mathrm{ttl}} & (a = \mathsf{Ttl}, u = q_t) \\ q_{\mathrm{par}} & (a = \mathsf{Par}, u = q_t) \\ q_{\mathrm{deadend}} & (\text{otherwise}), \quad\text{and} \end{cases}$$

$$F' = \{q_{\mathrm{doc}}\} \ .$$

and a DTD equivalent to this schema is as below:

```
<!ELEMENT Doc   (Sec*)>
<!ELEMENT Sec   (Ttl, par*, (Seg | Tpc)*)>
<!ELEMENT Seg   (Ttl, par*, (Seg | Tpc)*)>
<!ELEMENT Tpc   (Ttl, par*)>
<!ELEMENT Ttl   (#PCDATA)>
<!ELEMENT Par   (#PCDATA)>
```

Observe that this schema allows Sec nodes only as subordinates of the Doc node and that Tpc elements are not allowed to have surordinate Seg or Tpc elements. In other words, this schema is *minimally sufficient*.

6 Forestlog

Although this data model does not have tuples, it is possible to introduce an equivalent rule-based language called *forestlog*. We introduce forestlog only informally. The formal definition and the equivalence proof are left to the full paper.

The key idea is to impose three conditions so as to enable the conversion of a logic program into an algebraic query. Condition 1: each literal in the body of a standard rule has one and only one variable. Condition 2: the variable in a literal occurs only once in that literal. Condition 3: any variable in a standard rule must occur in some positive literal in the body and also occurs in the rule head.

A *variable* is an element of a countably infinite set **var**. An *intentional predicate* is the name of a relation instance computed by rules. An *extentional predicate* is the name of a relation instance stored in the database.

A *literal* is either:

- $S(u)$ or $\neg S(u)$ (positive literal or negative literal), where S is an extentional or intentional predicate and u is a forest over **label** and **var** $\cup$ **dom** in which only one variable occurs and it occurs once and only once, or
- $M(x)$ ("M matches x"), where M is the first parameter of the operator **select** and x is a variable.

A *rule head* is of the form $S(u)$, where S is an intentional predicate and u is either:

- a forest over **label** and **dom** $\cup$ **var**,
- $\mathbf{prod}(a, x, y)$, where a is a label, and x, y are variables,
- $\mathbf{rewrite}(a, i, v, x)$, where a, i, v are the first, second, third parameters of the operator **rewrite**, respectively, and x is a variable,
- $\mathbf{genrewrite}(a, v, x)$, where a and x are the first and second parameters of the operator **genrewrite**, respectively, and x is a variable,
- $\mathbf{mark}(a, \mathcal{C}, \mathcal{P}, x)$, where a, $\mathcal{C}$, $\mathcal{P}$ are the first, second, third parameters of the operator **mark**, respectively, and x is a variable.

A *rule* is either a *standard rule* or an *ad-hoc rule*. A standard rule is of the form *head* $\leftarrow A_1, A_2, \ldots, A_m$, where *head* is a rule head and $A_1, A_2, \ldots, A_m$ are literals. Any variable in the rule must occur in the rule head and must occur in some positive literal in the body.

An ad-hoc rule is of the form $S(x) \leftarrow A, R_1(y)$, where (1) S is an intentional predicate, (2) A is either $R_2(xy)$, $R_2(yx)$, or $\mathbf{subtree}(x, y)$ ("x is a subtree of y"), and (3) R_1, R_2 are intentional or extensional predicates.

A (non-recursive) *program* is a sequence of rules. More than one rule may have the same predicate in the head. Any intentional predicate used in the body of a rule must be defined by the preceding rules. The intentional predicate defined by the last rule is the *target predicate*. The semantic of programs, rules, head, and literals are defined in the obvious manner.

7   Conclusion

We have presented a data model that provides patterns and contextual conditions as well as schema transformation. Patterns and contextual conditions have been heavily used by SGML/XML transformation engines, while schema transformation is common in the database theory. But none of the previous works provides all three of patterns, contextual conditions, and schema transformation. We believe that this data model provides a theoretical foundation of future SGML/XML database systems.

However, there are many remaining issues. First, we do not really know if our operators are powerful enough. There might be some other useful operator that cannot be mimicked by our operators. Second, in order to perform pattern matching and contextual condition checking without scanning the entire document, we probably have to impose some restrictions on patterns and contextual conditions. Such restrictions help to provide index files for examining patterns and contextual conditions.

Acknowledgment I deeply appreciate Prof. Dirk Van Gucht for his extensive discussion and guidance during my stay in Indiana University. Prof. Ethan Munson and Mr. Paul Prescod gave me very helpful comments on an earlier version of this paper.

References

1. Abiteboul, S., Cluet, S., Milo, T.: Querying and updating the file. VLDB '93 **19** (1993) 73–84
2. Abiteboul, S., Hull, R., Vianu, V.: Foundations of Databases. Addison-Wesley (1995)
3. Baeza-Yates, R., Navarro, G.: Integrating contents and structure in text retrieval. SIGMOD Record **25:1** (1996) 67–79
4. Blake, G., Bray, T., Tompa, F.: Shortening the OED: Experience with a grammar-defined database. ACM TOIS **10:3** (1992) 213–232
5. Christophides, V., Abiteboul, S., Cluet, S., Scholl, M.: From structured documents to novel query facilities. SIGMOD Record **23:2** (1994) 313–324
6. Colby, L., Van Gucht, D., Saxton, L.: Concepts for modeling and querying list-structured data. Information Processing & Management **30:5** (1994) 687–709
7. Gécseg, F., Steinby, M.: Tree Automata. Akadémiai Kiadó (1984)
8. Gonnet, G., Tompa, F.: Mind your grammar: a new approach to modeling text. VLDB '87 **13** (1987) 339–346
9. Gyssens, M., Paredaens, J., Van Gucht, D.: A grammar-based approach towards unifying hierarchical data models. SIAM Journal on Computing **23:6** (1994) 1093–1137
10. Murata, M.: Transformation of documents and schemas by patterns and contextual conditions. Lecture Notes in Computer Science **1293** (1997) 153–169
11. Pair, C., Quere, A.: Définition et etude des bilangages réguliers. Information and Control **13:6** (1968) 565–593
12. Podelski, A.: A monoid approach to tree automata. In *Tree Automata and Languages* North-Holland (1992) 41–56
13. Takahashi, M.: Generalizations of regular sets and their application to a study of context-free languages. Information and Control **27** (1975) 1–36
14. Zdonik, S., Maier, D.: Readings in Object-Oriented Database Systems. Morgan Kaufmann (1990)

Springer
and the
environment

At Springer we firmly believe that an
international science publisher has a
special obligation to the environment,
and our corporate policies consistently
reflect this conviction.
We also expect our business partners –
paper mills, printers, packaging
manufacturers, etc. – to commit
themselves to using materials and
production processes that do not harm
the environment. The paper in this
book is made from low- or no-chlorine
pulp and is acid free, in conformance
with international standards for paper
permanency.

 Springer

Lecture Notes in Computer Science

For information about Vols. 1–1415

please contact your bookseller or Springer-Verlag